A SURVEY OF RUSSIAN MUSIC

BY

M. D. CALVOCORESSI

GREENWOOD PRESS, PUBLISHERS
WESTPORT, CONNECTICUT

Library of Congress Cataloging in Publication Data

Calvocoressi, Michel D   1877-1944.
    A survey of Russian music.

    Based on lectures delivered at Glasgow University as
Cramb lecturer for 1935.
    Reprint of the 1944 ed. published by Penguin Books,
Middlesex, Eng.
    1. Music, Russian--Addresses, essays, lectures.
I. Title.
ML300.C3 1974   781.7'47   73-6208
    ISBN 0-8371-6888-0

TO

" CORK "

(MRS. RICHARD CURLE)

IN AFFECTIONATE TRIBUTE TO

HER   WONDERFUL   KINDNESS

Chelsea, 1943

Originally published in 1944 by Penguin Books, Middlesex,
England

Reprinted with the permission of Penguin Books Ltd.

Reprinted in 1974 by Greenwood Press,
a division of Williamhouse-Regency Inc.

Library of Congress Catalogue Card Number 73-6208

ISBN 0-8371-6888-0

Printed in the United States of America

TO THE READER

In 1935 I was privileged to deliver a course of lectures on Russian music at Glasgow University as Cramb Lecturer for that session. I am greatly indebted to the trustees of the lectureship for their invitation, which compelled me to carry out a task that for many years had been both attracting and frightening me: that of inditing a reasonably thorough and fairly co-ordinated survey of the subject.

The special difficulties of the task are great. When dealing with the music of any other country, one may find guidance, or at least warnings against the more glaring forms of error, in the consensus of opinion reached, in the course of time, as to the character and value of most of the subject-matter, with a few exceptions in cases such as those, say, of Berlioz and Liszt, which seem fated to remain bones of contention to the end of time. But here almost everything is controversial. This peculiar situation, it is true, has at least one advantage: the critic may uphold his own convictions as uncompromisingly as he pleases without the fear that he may be flying in the face of unmistakable evidence, and with the feeling that his conclusions have at least an even chance of proving justified—as has already happened to those of us who were upholding Mussorgsky against his censors and revisers in the early days of the campaign around him.

This is not, and does not pretend to be, an unprejudiced survey. All I can say is that I did not yield to my prejudices precipitately, having been made fully aware of them by the protests some of my views aroused—e.g., by indignation meetings held in Russia and elsewhere (some of them in my presence) on the subject of my attitude to Tchaikovsky's music. I do not believe criticism can be objective, or even impartial. The last few years have seen, in this country, the collapse of a strenuous attempt, by one of our most expert and dexterous critics, to establish that it can, and should, be objective—a notion that he seems to have given up for good and all.

Analysis, of course, can be objective up to a point: yet, even the act of selecting and emphasizing certain features of the works analysed implies a subjective decision—in other words, a judgment: it means they are considered material in some way or other.

In the lectures, which were for students, I strove to achieve a measure of objectivity by quoting and comparing conflicting judgments—notably on Tchaikovsky, Scriabin, Taneief, and Stravinsky, and on general questions such as the rights and wrongs of musical nationalism in its various aspects, of programme-music, and so forth. But this procedure—the only sound one when education of the mind and taste is the object—would have made too heavy going in a book intended for the music-loving public, who require a modicum of advice, free from perturbing dilemmas. I found it advisable, however, to resort to it in certain difficult cases.

Apart from that, this book contains all the substance of my lectures, practically unaltered except that I have reduced the technicalities to a bare minimum and crowded them, so far as possible, into one chapter. I have considerably extended the section referring to Soviet music, although not as much by far as I should have liked to do: far too little of this music is procurable at present. The same is true, unfortunately, of the works of Russian composers now living in other countries. I am fully aware that on these two subjects I have given far too little apart from nomenclature. I trust that this little will at least be found useful when normal circumstances again prevail and the moment comes to consider what to perform and what to listen to.

I have to acknowledge my indebtedness to many friends and colleagues: first and foremost, among those that are no more, to Professor Nikolai Findeisen and Andrei Rimsky-Korsakof, from whose writings I have learnt much, and who assisted me most generously and indefatigably, never leaving a query unanswered however great the labour entailed; and also to Grigory Timofeief and Viatcheslav Karatyghin. Among the living, to Professors George Khubov, Victor Belaief, and Paul Lamm. The last named, in his capacity as editor of Mussorgsky's collected works in their genuine form (Russian State Editions), has done more than anybody else to remedy the most appalling injustice in the whole history of music.

All the facts in Chapter II, and most of the facts in Chapter III, which I am sure will be found the most useful of all, were taken from Findeisen's *Précis of Russian Music Until the End of the Eighteenth Century*, and Stolpiansky's *Music in Old Petersburg*; and I claim no credit except for disseminating a few scraps of the information contained in those books, both of which—and especially Findeisen's admirable *Précis*—should long since have been made available in a translation.

In this country, I am indebted to my friend Gerald Abraham, whose alert, spirited, wisely balanced studies of Russian music have confirmed certain of my views, completed certain others, and covered much fresh ground with exemplary lucidity and thoroughness; and, last but not least, to Professor W. G. Whittaker, whose advice and practical help in the matter of preparing and illustrating the lectures proved invaluable.

Reluctantly, I decided against giving a list of records. There would have been too many gaps in it. For instance, not one record of Mussorgsky's *Boris Godunof* in its genuine text seems to exist. And certain of the recorded readings that I know of other works are of a kind that might go far towards giving a bad name to Russian music.

BIBLIOGRAPHICAL NOTE

A.   Principal Books in English

Abraham, G., *Studies in Russian Music*.   London, 1935.

Abraham, G., *On Russian Music*.   London, 1939.

Abraham, G., *Eight Soviet Composers*.   London, 1943.

Belaief, V., *Boris Godunof in its New Version*.   London, 1928.

Blom, E., *Tchaikovsky's Orchestral Works*.   London, 1927.

Boelza, E., *Handbook of Soviet Musicians*.   London, 1943.

Calvocoressi, M. D., and Abraham, G., *Masters of Russian Music*.   London, 1936.

Cobbett's *Cyclopedic Survey of Chamber Music*.   London, 1929.

Evans, E., *Tchaikovsky*,   London, 1935.

Grove's *Dictionary of Music and Musicians*; 3rd edition and Supplement.

Montagu-Nathan, E., *Contemporary Russian Composers*.   London, 1917.

Rimsky-Korsakof, N., *Memoirs of my Musical Life*.   New York and London, 1942.

B.   Russian Sources

An adequate bibliography is out of the question.   A fairly comprehensive one is given in *Masters of Russian Music*.

CONTENTS

A SURVEY OF RUSSIAN MUSIC

CHAPTER I

THE SUBJECT OUTLINED

WHY does the term " Russian music " imply something more special than just music that happens to have been composed in Russia and by Russians, and is simply part and parcel of the music composed throughout the world at large? The reply is that Russian music, and especially the best nineteenth-century Russian music, has strongly marked national features which do make it something special and apart.

Indeed, ever since Russian music began to spread outside Russia, theorists have been discussing the problem of nationality in music from a variety of angles—for instance: is national music different, in any essential respect, from non-national? And, whether it is or not, which are its merits and demerits? With regard to our present subject, there is no need to go far afield in order to reply to all such questions: Russian national music owes much to the influence of native folk-music, and also of Eastern music. Thence a number of purely musical features that are outside the tradition and usage of the music of Western civilization. So, the important point is not the abstract fact that a great proportion of Russian music is national, but the thoroughly concrete fact that it has a distinctive physiognomy of its own, and proceeds in directions hitherto unknown to modern Western music. Much of what at first was particular to it is now merged in the universal vocabulary and technique of musical art. This precludes all possibility of dismissing the innovations of the great Russians as barbaric, crude, and valueless to art, as was the fashion among pundits in the days, not so far back, when Russian music was so little known that anybody who revealed even a modicum of familiarity with the works of Mussorgsky, Balakiref, or Borodin, was regarded as possessing more or less esoteric knowledge, and would probably have been dubbed a highbrow had that ridiculous term been invented. By now, the music of these and other Russian masters has gained a place in the world's repertory, and many excellent judges have paid tribute to its merits. On the other hand, there are a few competent, and indeed distinguished, critics who dismiss it casually, wondering why (as one of them puts it)

11

anybody should trouble " to discuss it as if it was as important as that of the older civilizations, and to study it as if it was in the same category as Beethoven's ".

This, obviously, is overlooking the fact that no æsthetic judgment is valid unless based on exhaustive unprejudiced study. But if nowadays there is, in certain quarters, a tendency to relegate lovers of national Russian music to the " low-brow " category (and that is what the saying I quoted amounts to); and if, elsewhere, a certain weariness is felt (all the more accountable for the reason that not all Russian music is first-rate, and much of that which is first-rate remains all too little known), this should be regarded, it might seem, as a symptom of that reaction against the immediate past which is never lacking in musical life, is usually short-lived, does not go very deep, and, all told, clears the air and does more good than harm.

In order to understand how this music came to be something apart and unique, it suffices to turn to its history.

The art of composition was born in Russia under highly particular circumstances, the like of which is nowhere else to be observed. Russia is a vast country into which modern civilization penetrated late, a country peopled with many races, Slavonic, Finnish, Varangian, Turanian, and others, with strong Eastern currents permeating it. For many centuries it had no musical culture in the usual sense of the term. What musical culture it acquired was the privilege of a small fraction of the aristocracy, was imported from other countries —Italy, France, Germany, and Britain—and was kept alive by foreign artists only. The people had nothing to do with what is called " art " music—that is, the music turned out by composers for the benefit of a more or less cultured public: but they had their native music, an enormous variety of folk-songs and dance-tunes constituting a live and flourishing tradition. And this folk-music always had a hold upon the educated classes as well as upon the illiterate masses. So that when the art of composition began to crop up in Russia, those who went in for it had neither the advantages nor the drawbacks of a hereditary tradition of their own behind them.

Their background was, on the one hand, the examples imported from abroad, from which they had to learn all about art-forms, resources, and technical processes; and on the other hand, the native music that surrounded them and was to them an everyday language, a close and live reality, a tradition that led in a direction which inborn, deep-rooted impulses prompted them to follow. Their problem, therefore, was to effect an adjustment between these two driving forces. What the actual terms of the problem were, and how they solved it, will be shown in a further chapter.

However important background, atmosphere, and other circumstances may be, only with the coming of men of genius can musical composition flourish in any country. In Russia, this essential condition was first fulfilled with the coming of Glinka (1804–1857). Balakiref, Borodin, Mussorgsky, and Rimsky-Korsakof followed. Their genius was oriented in a thoroughly national direction. Tchaikovsky's music was no less Russian in character than theirs, but in a different way, standing closer to that of the West.

Balakiref once said to a French critic who had explained to him that in France, Tchaikovsky was regarded as cosmopolitan, and not Russian: " How strange! He is profoundly Russian. If our native music did not have the same hold on him as it had on us, it is because he did not grow up in thoroughly Russian surroundings: his mother was French, and his nurse German, whereas we were nurtured on folk-tunes from babyhood on."

This makes it clear enough that it was not arbitrarily and wilfully that most of the Russian masters went in for nationalism. They did not seek in their native music means of achieving ostentatious originality or revolting against tradition: they simply composed as Russians and for the Russians. Borodin often expressed astonishment that his music should be making headway abroad. " *Igor*," he wrote to a friend, " being fundamentally a national opera, can hardly interest anybody other than us Russians." Mussorgsky was amazed to hear that Liszt admired his *Nursery* songs, " those portrayals of purely Russian children ".

So, Russian music progressed for a time on national lines, in the teeth of fierce opposition, the leader of which was Anton Rubinstein, the famous pianist and founder of the Petersburg Conservatoire (opened in 1862). Rubinstein went proclaiming that art should be universal, and attempts to write national music, beginning with Glinka's, were doomed to failure.

Others, while not sharing Rubinstein's blind prejudice, preferred to keep closer to Western usage and even Western conventions. And, on the other hand, a time came when the national movement spent itself, for the reason that there were no newcomers of genius to carry it further; a routine of composing on national lines—or rather, national stereotypes—developed, as was bound to happen. So the character of Russian music went on changing gradually; the national element either became a matter of mere surface aspect and colour or was entirely lacking, and a definitely non-national school came into being.

Shortly afterwards, Stravinsky (*b.* 1882) appeared, and for a while revived the nationalist tradition, afterwards proceeding, however, in very different directions. And after the 1917 upheaval, with the advent of the Soviet régime, an altogether new epoch began. Like all other human activities, composition had to comply with the dictates of Soviet ideology and policy instead of remaining governed by the composers' impulses and calculations: again an unheard-of state of things, which compels us to regard Soviet music as something special and apart. One noteworthy consequence of this revolution was that nationalism not only came into favour again, but was painstakingly fostered by the government, far-reaching measures being taken to encourage composers to study and assimilate the native music of all the races within the Union.

The amazing thing is that all this happened within less than a century. Glinka's first opera, *A Life for the Tsar*, which ushered Russian national music into the world, was first produced in November 1836. Forty years later, Balakiref, Mussorgsky, Borodin, Tchaikovsky, and Rimsky-Korsakof had already given much of their best. Stravinsky's first big work, *The Fire-Bird*, came in 1910. The year 1926 saw the first performance of Shostakovitch's symphony in F minor, a work that gave him pride of place among the composers who started their career under the Soviet régime. In January 1936, the banning of his opera *The Lady Macbeth of Mtsensk*, which two years before had been hailed as a masterpiece and held up as a consummate example of the Soviet spirit in opera, came to show how strong a hold Soviet ideology and policy had gained.

Such is the history of Russian music. It is striking and unusual enough to be worth studying for its own sake. Its ultimate interest, of course, lies in the value of the music that illustrates its various phases, and upon their value, not as mere pleasure-giving or curiosity-rousing exceptions, but as legitimate artistic currency, standing on a par with that of all other countries—upon their value from both the æsthetic and the spiritual point of view.

Russian music came into being at a moment when, with the advent of romanticism, new perspectives had opened to human thought. In the musical field Berlioz, Chopin, Schumann, Liszt, and Wagner were at work, and the need to extend the vocabulary, technique, and range of the art made itself acutely felt. As regards vocabulary and technique, this could be done either by exploiting further and further the possibilities of the current idiom and processes, or by seeking resources elsewhere.

It was inevitable that the former course should eventually beget an increasingly overladen and complicated style.   Richard Strauss's is a case in point:

> The board groans under a weight of incongruous dainties. We are sated before the feast is over, and think ourselves fortunate if we escape with our digestions unimpaired.   There can be no doubt about the wealth: it cries out to us from every corner.   And yet, we should have been better off with plainer living and higher thinking.   All this bears the mark of a decadent and sophisticated art.
>
> (Hadow on Strauss, in *Collected Essays*, London, 1928).

Moreover, under the influence of romanticism, music, like all the other arts, besides striving to break the bonds of classical usage, was tending to become overburdened with philosophical and symbolic ambitions.   An epidemic of solemnity and turgescence threatened.   A point was even reached at which obscurity and pretentiousness came to be regarded, in certain quarters, as merits rather than as defects.   Complications of idiom and processes such as those to which Hadow refers were symptomatic of this frame of mind.

Of course, it was much later that the evil became apparent, but the germ was there when the Russians appeared on the scene.   It was, indeed, inherent in the romanticism of the 'thirties and 'forties, most of whose exponents took art, and also themselves, in desperate earnest, light-heartedness and simplicity of tone being gradually relegated to the lighter forms of art.

The great merit of the Russian national masters was, as Gerald Abraham has put it, their " essential *naïveté* ", the main value of their contributions to art lying " in their thorough freshness of outlook, in their starting again—sometimes in a new direction—from the first principles ".   They found new sources of inspiration in their surroundings, in their country's scenery, history, legends, and everyday life—in those provinces of reality and fancy that were Russia's own, in all that had come to her from the East.   It is especially characteristic of this spirit that, for them, even the goblins, demigods, and monsters of Slavonic mythology should have been neither symbols, nor period-pieces, nor pretexts for romantic flourishes; that they should have taken the world of pure fancy as a reality accepted on its own terms and for its own sake, and enjoyed it with child-like whole-heartedness and thoroughly mature artistic consciousness.

There are glimpses of this kind of thing in the fantastic scenes in

Weber's operas, in Mendelssohn's *Midsummer Night's Dream* music, in Berlioz's *Queen Mab* scherzo. The Russians went much farther. In Glinka's opera *Ruslan and Liudmila,* for instance, we are invited to take quite seriously the tale of a young princess kidnapped by a wizard on the day of her betrothal, and of her rescue—which involves, among other episodes, a fight with a giant head that stands, like a sphinx, in the middle of a desert. One of Rimsky-Korsakof's operas, *Snow-Maiden,* is the story of a girl who was really a snowflake, and who melted away as soon as warmed by the glow of sunlight and of love. In another, *Tsar Saltan,* a young hero whom a fairy protects defeats the wicked plots of his mother's enemies by turning into a bumble-bee which stings them every time they tell a lie. In the instrumental music, we encounter tone-poems inspired by the legend of a merchant-minstrel's wonderful adventures in the kingdom under the sea (Rimsky-Korsakof's *Sadko*), by tales from the *Arabian Nights* (his *Sheherazade*), or simply by the forest of fairy-land with its nymphs and water-sprites and goblins and giants. Balakiref's *Song of the Golden Fish* and Borodin's song *The Queen of the Sea* are songs of sirens trying to entice a passer-by. There are many such songs in the Western repertory, notably Liszt's *Lorelei*: but they are all descriptions from outside, in which we perceive the poet and the composer speaking. With Balakiref and Borodin, we hear no voice but that of the siren.

Many such comparisons, either of a general or of a technical order, will be needed to make clear how much that was new and far-reaching is to be found in the national Russian music. Naturally, no question arises of pitting this music against any other: the one point is to show that (to quote Mr. Abraham again) " the Russian masters' freedom from preconceptions opened the way to all sorts of curious triumphs ", and that they gave the world a wealth not only of splendid music, but of music of a kind that no other composers were thinking of turning out at the time.

CHAPTER II

THE EARLY HISTORY OF MUSIC IN RUSSIA

It is a striking fact that the earliest reference we have to the music of the country that is now Russia should appear to stress the contrast between the barbarity of that music and the orderliness and elegance of the music of a civilized country. It occurs in an old Greek ode, which says: "Friends, let us not with shouts and braying imitate the Scythians in their revels, but drink our wine quietly to the sound of beautiful hymns."

So far as this passage may be taken to refer to music and not to behaviour only, it bears a striking resemblance to what the German composer Hugo Wolf wrote in 1885 of Balakiref's *Islamey*:

> That wild Balakiref! What a music-cannibal! He is not content with murdering music: he must gloat upon the corpse he has dismembered in his mad composing moods;

and with this, from Edward Dannreuther's pen in the *Oxford History of Music*, 1905:

> Mussorgsky appears wilfully eccentric. His music impresses the Western ear as barbarously ugly. He deliberately chooses Oriental barbarisms for barbaric ends.

Of the music of the Scythians Sarmatians, and other forebears of the Russians, we know nothing except that it did exist. Plutarch, in his *Ethica*, mentions that long before his time, hyperborean priests visited Delos, bringing with them flutes, fifes, and cithers. Elsewhere, he refers to Scythian instruments made of bone or of wood. A second-century A.D. dictionary, the work of the grammarian Julius Polydeuces, mentions a Scythian harp or lute with five strings, and also flutes made of the bones of eagles and kites.

Several Greek historians, quoted in Karamzin's *History of Russia*, say that at the end of the sixth century A.D., the Greeks, at war with their northern neighbours, captured three men who were carrying not weapons, but simply cithers (*i.e. gusli*, the Slavonic equivalent of the cither). They explained that they were Slavs, had come from the far end of the Western ocean (*i.e.* the Baltic), and were not soldiers, but just musicians.

In the tenth century, at Byzantium, the emperor Constantine Porphyrogenitus had in his service Slavonic players, whose duty it was to attend the theatre whenever public games took place. These, after the hyperborean priests who visited Delos, must have been the very earliest ambassadors of Russian music in other countries.

Other evidence is provided by sculptures, frescoes, and similar monuments, as well as by writers of different periods. In the tenth century an Arabian, Akhmet Ibn Fadlan, who visited the Bulgarian settlements on the banks of the Volga, described the funeral of a Bulgarian of high rank. The ceremony, he says, included a good deal of singing, and a musical instrument was placed in the tomb. Another writer of the same period, Omar Ibn Dasta, mentions various string and wind instruments used by the Slavs of Kooyaf, or Kief.

This evidence makes it clear that the country had its native music, and that musical culture came to it from the south and the east: first from Greece and Rome, then from Byzantium and from the Arabs, spreading, towards the tenth century or so, among the Bulgarians, along the banks of the Volga and among all the Southern Slavs. At that time, there existed typically national Russian instruments, different from those in use elsewhere that came to be imported. These were, in all likelihood, similar to those to which earlier sources refer, and practically identical with plucked string and wind instruments still in use among the Russian people. And while foreign influences were beginning to make themselves felt, native music continued to pursue its own course.

No actual example of primitive Russian music is known, but there seems to be, in many folk-songs preserved and sung to the present day, internal evidence that they hark back to heathen Russia. Countless references to the old mythological deities occur, and also much that would be meaningless except in connection with sun-worship, tree-worship, and so on. As to the music, all that could be said would be merely conjectural. It is clear enough, however, that archaic features are present in many of those folk-tunes. Two of the tunes regarded by Professor Findeisen as most typical in this respect are given in Example I at the end of this book.

But, during all these centuries and long after, no art-forms, even rudimentary, seem to have been evolved from that folk-music. Art-forms, in proportions as they appeared, were importations from abroad.

Russia, until the twelfth century, consisted of a number of independent, democratic states, each of them ruled by a *Kniaz* (*i.e.* duke, or prince). The most important and most civilized of these was Kief, whose history begins in the ninth century. It was then that musical notation was first imported into Russia, together with Byzantine church music. And it was then, too, that begins, so far as we know, the history of the *Skomorokhi*, the Russian jesters and actors who gave shows, sang, danced, and played a variety of musical instruments. The first mention we have of them occurs in Nestor's *Chronicle* (1068), which describes them as " messengers of the devil, who turn the peoples' mind away from God with their songs and trumpets and games ". The music they played or sang must have been thoroughly vernacular. No actual specimen of it has come to us. They were in existence until the middle of the seventeenth century, when an edict of the Russian Church, confirmed by edicts from the secular authorities, prohibited " their satanic songs and instrumental playing, and the diabolic games with which they depraved the people ". It is held by certain experts that, driven away from the cities, some of them found refuge in the distant parts of the Muscovite empire, where they continued to ply their trade; and that tunes from their repertory are extant to the present day, incorporated in the folk-tunes of those regions.

In 1169, Kief was plundered and practically destroyed. Novgorod then became the centre of civilization. The Novgorod period was one of assimilation and elaboration, which laid the foundations of a national Russian culture. Its legends and ballads tell of many heroes who included musicianship among their superhuman gifts. One was Vassili (or Vaska) Buslaef, of whom it was said: " When he reached the age of seven, his loving mother had him educated. He studied letters and sciences, learnt to write with a pen and to sing Church music. And today you would find in all Novgorod no singer comparable to him." This Buslaef was no mere creature of legend. He existed in actual fact, and in 1171 was burgomaster of Novgorod.

Then there was Sadko, whose story Rimsky-Korsakof has evoked in a tone-poem, and later in an opera. The legend says that he was a rich merchant, and also a professional singer and player of the *gusli*, who one day was thrown into the sea as a sacrifice to the King of the Ocean, in whose realm he had, thanks to his musical skill, wonderful adventures. Sadko, too, actually existed. He was a merchant and minstrel. It is recorded that in 1167 he built a stone church and dedicated it to St. Basil and St. Gleb. Dobrynia Nikititch, whose name appears in many folk-ballads, lived in the late tenth century. He was a councillor of Duke Vladimir of Kief, became burgomaster of Novgorod, and won fame with his singing and playing. There is plenty of other evidence to show that music was held in high honour in old Novgorod.

Towards the end of the fifteenth century, Moscow became the centre of Russian civilization. The Muscovite period was the dawn of a national, and no longer merely regional, Russian culture. Relations with other countries were considerably extended, especially with Italy and Germany, and with Turkey and Bokhara in Asia; and music benefited considerably thereby. The Grand Duke Ivan III married a Greek princess, Sophia Paleologos, who set the fashion for musical entertainments. In 1490 an organist, Johan Salvator by name, was brought to Moscow by her brother, and created a big impression. A Court chapel consisting of about thirty-five singers was founded. Ivan the Terrible (1533–1584) was fond of folk-music, of church music, and of the musical entertainments provided by the *Skomorokhi*. He brought church-singers and entertainers to Moscow. In 1550 or so, he ordered that the Court chapel should practise part-singing as practised in Western countries.

In 1586 an envoy from Queen Elizabeth of England, Sir Jerome Horsey, brought to Tsar Feodor, Ivan's son, presents which included organs and virginals (and, for Boris Godunof, the Protector of the Realm, a dappled bull, mastiffs, and lions). In his relation of his journey (London 1598) he says that " the emporis his [Boris Godunof's] sister admired especially at the organs and vergenalls, all gilt and enambled. My men that plaid upon them were much made of, and admitted into such presence often where myself could not come."

During the brief reign of Dimitri the Impostor (1605–1606) Western (mainly Polish) music gained a further footing at Court under the influence of his Polish consort, Marina. Both vernacular and foreign music were included in the informal entertainments that took place in the palace of Tsar Mikhail Feodorovitch (1613–1645); and distinguished organists came to Moscow from Germany and Poland. Interest in organ music grew, not only at Court, but in aristocratic circles. And music was practised in the foreign colonies that flourished in the capital.

More important events marked the reign of Tsar Alexis Mikhailovitch (1645–1676). Relations with the West grew closer, and culture spread more rapidly. As it happened, a close friend of the Tsar, Artamon Matveyef, had married a Scotswoman, Hamilton by name, who was fond of music. In their home, the Tsar learnt to enjoy the music of Western civilization. In 1672 a Court Theatre came into being. The repertory included plays with songs by foreign composers (but principally by a certain Gregory, the pastor of the Saxon Church at Moscow) and Schütz's ballet *Orfeo*. Apparently, when the Tsar first saw this ballet, he expressed the wish that it be performed without the music, which he found too new-fangled, and in certain respects heathenish. Upon being told that it would not be possible to dance without music, he graciously conceded the point. And as early as 1671, on the Tsarevitch Feodor's birthday, the boyars and ladies performed at the Court a comedy, *Tur* (the name of an old God), with Slavonic and Caucasian songs and Polish dances. Two other plays of the same type were given that year. These must have pleased the Tsar, the music not striking so new-fangled nor, despite the mythological elements in the plays, so heathenish a note.

Peter the Great (1686–1725), the founder of the new Europeanized Russia, had no interest in music other than that of the Church. Not so, however, his entourage, many members of which learnt to enjoy opera and concerts during their visits abroad. So (the Tsar being gifted with a keen sense of expediency) music was occasionally given a place at Court. Many actors and musicians were brought from abroad.

Moscow was given its first public theatre in 1702. Public performances of band music also began to take place.

As soon as St. Petersburg was founded (1703) it became the main centre of musical life. The Empress and a number of noblemen had their private orchestras and choirs. During the reign of the Empress Anna (1730–1740) music made far more headway in the new capital. Foreign musicians came in numbers, and many settled there. Anna kept both a foreign orchestra, whose conductor was Francisco Araja, a Neapolitan, and an orchestra of native instrumentalists. Harpsichord players were in great demand. Araja (who exercised a considerable influence) was only one of the many foreign composers who came to work in Russia: other notable ones were Hermann Raupach, Giovanni Madonis, Galuppi, Lolli, Viotti, and A. F. Titz. Performances at court of Italian operas began in 1735. The Empress Elizabeth (1741–1761) loved both Western music and native folk-music, and was fond of singing folk-songs or joining in choral singing. The Russian theatre she founded was the first to be devoted to the production of regular stage plays. During her reign, the fashion for Italian music prevailed.

Catherine the Great (1762–1796) favoured Italian music only. But while foreign art was gaining ground, interest in folk-tunes (the earliest printed collections of which appeared during her reign) was growing steadily; and the first Russian composers, beginning with Pashkevitch and Khandoshkin, appeared.

During all these years, music made little progress outside the court and the aristocracy. The middle classes and the people did not participate in these entertainments of the wealthy. The first public concert in St. Petersburg was given in a private house, in July 1746, by a German singer. Another took place in 1748 at the home of Prince Gagarin, press notices announcing that " concerts in the Italian, English, and Dutch style would be played; there would be singing in Italian, German, Dutch and English; the price of admittance was one rouble; gentlemen, merchants, and other respectable people were invited to attend, but drunken lackeys and idle women would be refused admittance ".

Concerts were few until 1769, when they became more frequent. The first Russian artist to give a concert was Khandoshkin, in 1780. In Moscow, regular public concerts were instituted in 1780; the first public performance of an opera took place in 1777.

During the last quarter of the eighteenth century the practice of music developed considerably. Not only players and teachers, but the dealers and publishers who cropped up benefited thereby. Wealthy people began to have their private orchestras of serfs, consisting, as a rule, of eight or ten players. Towards the end of the century, ingenious conductors made a business of building up such orchestras and selling them ready trained, with their families thrown in.

Some of these orchestras consisted of Russian horns, each giving out one note only; their length varied from 3 to 98 inches. The first orchestra of that kind was organized by the Czech horn-player Mares, shortly after 1750, for Naryshkin, the Master of the Imperial Hunt and Director of the Court Theatre. The fashion spread, and endured until 1830 or thereabouts. In 1821 the Grand Duke Constantine presented the Duke of Saxe-Coburg-Gotha with one that consisted of 300 players, and whose repertory included Mozart symphonies and overtures, and works by Haydn. Folk-tune arrangements had their place in the repertory of these orchestras.

Interest in chamber-music was developing. The Empress Catherine had in her service a small chamber ensemble, led by Anton-Ferdinand Titz, which gave concerts during card-parties. Several noblemen followed suit. One of the earliest examples of chamber-music inscribed to a Russian patron was the set of six sonatas for violin and harpsichord, " dédiées à Monsieur le Prince Dimitry de Galitzine " by Raupach (published in Paris, 1766). As early as 1738 the Venetian Madonis had inscribed to the Empress Anna twelve so-called " symphonies " for violin and bass. He is said to have composed instrumental music (so far unidentified) on Russian and Ukrainian tunes. The first Russian to make his mark as a composer of chamber-music was Ivan Khandoshkin (c. 1740–1804), whose output includes sonatas for two violins and sets of variations on Russian folk-tunes for the same combination or for violin solo.   And the first to give a concert of his own compositions was Danilo Kashin (176?–1841).   The event took place at Moscow in March 1790.   The works were a piano concerto and an overture, the programme being eked out with " arias by the best composers, sung by one of Kashin's pupils ".

Nothing of this, however, amounted to much so far as regards the actual prehistory of Russian music proper.   The most important point is that while foreign music and musicians were beginning to spread musical culture and fashions, native folk-music, instead of receding into the background, was holding its own in all classes of society, and even gaining here and there a certain amount of ground. But, on the other hand, very little interest·was taken in the achievements of Russian artists.   Indeed, as Stolpiansky says, the attitude of the public to native composers and players was a patronizing, condescending one: " they were mere curiosities and freaks, whereas those who came from abroad were celebrities and great artists.   After giving his concerts, the Italian Lolli would be presented with a diamond-studded bow, but a meagre recompense in money was considered sufficient for the brilliant Russian Khandoshkin."

CHAPTER III

OPERA AND THE DAWN OF RUSSIAN MUSIC

OPERA, from the first, was the genre that attracted Russian music-lovers most. It is said that attendance at Court concerts was compulsory: but no similar regulation was ever found needful so far as regarded opera performances. According to Findeisen, what first gave rise to the notion of having operas performed in Russian was the success scored, in 1750, by a Russian singer, Poltarasky by name, in an Italian opera by the Court chapel-master, Araja. There was, at the time, no native composer capable of providing an opera score; so the task devolved on Araja. This first opera in Russian, entitled *Cephalos and Procris*, was produced in 1755.

The following year, a one-act operetta, *Taniusha*, with music arranged by a certain Volkof, was produced at Moscow. Not a trace of it remains; and nothing but the libretto of a comic opera, *Aniuta*, the music by an unidentified composer, produced at Court in 1772, is extant.

Thus was Russian opera ushered into the world, modestly falling into place alongside the foreign operas performed at Court and elsewhere by Italian, German, and French companies; and also at least one English company, which came to Petersburg in 1771-1772 and produced, among other things, Dibdin's *The Padlock*, Arne's *Love in a Village*, and Arnold's *Maid of the Mill*. As Findeiser points out, the repertory of these companies included light and comic operas of a popular, often plebeian nature, showing contemporary characters in scenes of everyday life; these set Russian composers a far more useful example than the stereotypes, mythological or other, of grand opera.

Soon, foreign composers—Kerzelli, Bulant, Raupach, and others —began to turn out operas " à la Russe ", or at least on Russian subjects, in increasing numbers. Two of these composers, the Baron Wanzura and Franz Xavier Blyma (17?-1822), were, Findeisen tells us, Slavs (probably Czechs), and so better capable of understanding the idiosyncrasies of Russian folk-tunes and using them without distorting them almost beyond recognition: whereas an Italian composer would think nothing of altering, for instance, the rhythm of a Russian peasant dance tune into that of a Court minuet. Indeed, Blyma (to whom Findeisen is the first to have given the place which he deserves) availed himself of vernacular tunes and

24

turns to excellent purpose in his opera *Old-World Christmas* (1799), notably of the well-known " Slava! " (" Glory be! ") used by Beethoven in the third movement of his Razumovsky quartet (op. 59, no 2), by Mussorgsky in the coronation scene in *Boris Godunof*, and later by several other Russians. Blyma gave it the form of a very effective aria with chorus. But, Findeisen continues, the foundations of the genuine national style that was to come into being in the following century was really laid by three Russians: Mikhail Matinsky (175?-1820), Vassily Pashkevitch (17?-17?), and Evstignei Fomin (1761-1800). All three were of plebeian extraction. Matinsky was born a serf; so was Kashin, whom his master, after having had him trained by Sarti, liberated in 1799, and who in the 19th century (he died at a ripe old age in 1841) did much to popularize folk-tunes by his arrangements of them for home and concert use. Fomin was the son of a private soldier. He and Matinsky were educated in Italy.

Two operas in the music of which characteristically national elements appear were produced in 1779: *The Miller who was a Wizard, a Deceiver, and a Marriage Broker* at Moscow, and *The Saint Petersburg Bazaar* at St. Petersburg. So far as can be ascertained, the music of the former was composed by a Moscow violinist, Sokolovsky by name, but shortly afterwards revised by Fomin. Only the revised form has reached us: so, it is to Fomin that the credit for the many merits of this score goes.

The same happened with *The Saint Petersburg Bazaar*: the music was originally provided by Matinsky, but remodelled by Pashkevitch, and only the remodelled version is extant. Thus, at the very beginning of the history of Russian opera, we are confronted with a state of things identical with that which long obtained with regard to Mussorgsky's *Boris Godunof* and *Khovanshchina*, when it was impossible to know how much of these was the work of Mussorgsky and how much that of Rimsky-Korsakof (see Chapters VII and VIII), unless one was able to gain access to the genuine unrevised texts.[1] The main points of interest in these two scores are : in *The Miller*, a high level of technique, freshness of style, a genuine sense of colour, the skilful and appropriate use of folk-tunes ; in *The Bazaar*, fairly successful attempts at musical characterization, and a good deal of music (chiefly choral) of genuinely vernacular character. The wedding-eve scene in it, we are told, constitutes the first attempt to create an atmosphere of national tradition in opera. Pashke-

---

[1] And it is characteristic of the difficulties historians have to cope with that the above facts should have remained unknown until Findeisen called attention to them in 1928.

vitch is at his best in his legendary comic opera *Fevei* (1786), the peasant opera *Fedul and his Children* (composed in collaboration with Vincent Martin y Soler, a Spaniard who settled in St. Petersburg in 1788), and in the three choruses he provided for the opera *Oleg* (1790). This was the joint work of three composers, the other two being the Italians Cannobio and Sarti. It is interesting to note that in the score Sarti resorted—rather stiffly and self-consciously it is true —to the old Greek modes.

The libretti of *Oleg, Fedul,* and *Fevei* were written by the Empress Catherine. Other libretti from her pen were *Voyeslavitch the Novgorod Bogatyr* (hero) and *Kossometovitch the Sorry Bogatyr*. These, like *Fevei,* were prototypes of the libretti based on old native legends and fables, or on imitation of these, that found great favour with nineteenth-century national composers. The former was set to music by Fomin, so far as can be ascertained (the score is lost); and the latter by Vincent Martin y Soler. A more characteristic example is the libretto *The Bold Brave Knight Akhrideitch,* in which several typical characters of Russian fairy-tales play a part. It was set to music by Baron Ernest Wanzura (1750–1801), an amateur in matters technical, but endowed with a certain feeling for national colour. The score, in all likelihood, was knocked into shape by some professional or other.

These few summary indications show the trend of events during the last decades of the eighteenth century. It may be added that in the instrumental works of Bortniansky (1751–1825; a gifted and industrious composer, remembered chiefly on account of his church music) and especially in his keyboard sonatas, published in 1783–1784, Findeisen has discovered a sufficient number of vernacular elements to justify his being included in the list of precursors of the national style.

At the beginning of the nineteenth century, the Venetian composer and conductor Cavos (1776–1840) settled in Russia. He was genuinely interested in Russian native music, and did his utmost to introduce at least echoes of it in his operas. His first exploit was to transform a German *Singspiel* entitled *Donauweibchen* (The Danube Sprite) into a " Russian " opera by the simple expedient of altering names and settings and introducing a few popular Russian tunes into the score. The success of the venture gave him the idea of composing operas on genuine Russian legendary and historical subjects: notably *Ilya the Bogatyr* (1806), *Dobrynia Nikititch* (1818), *The Fire-Bird, Svietlana* (both 1822), *The Youth of Ivan the Third* (1823), and, in 1815, *Ivan Sussanin,* the libretto of which was based on the story of the heroic peasant who gave his life to save that of Tsar Michael Romanof—the story that became the subject of Glinka's *A Life for the Tsar.*

As a composer he displayed competence but little originality. As a conductor, he rendered yeoman's service to the art. And when Glinka came forth with *A Life for the Tsar,* he generously devoted all his energies to ensuring a fine production for the work.

The outcome of the Napoleonic wars was a great outbreak of national feeling, which had its influence on music as well as on literature. Indeed, the story of nineteenth-century Russian music and that of nineteenth-century Russian literature are strikingly similar. Until the end of the eighteenth century, Russia had no original literature to speak of except her traditional epics, legends, tales, and lyric poems. Then Pushkin came, and after him Gogol, Lermontof, Turgenief, Dostoievsky, and all the other writers who found inspiration in national lore and national reality; exactly as Glinka came, to be followed by the great nationalists commonly (and absurdly) called " the Five " outside Russia, and in Russia the *Kutchka,* or " mighty handful ", and by others grouped around them or following in their footsteps.

It is symptomatic of the new national trend that as early as 1812 Stepan Degtiaref, one of the most active and gifted composers of that time, should have composed an oratorio, *The Liberation of Moscow* (*from the Poles* in 1613), and begun work on another, *Napoleon's Flight,* which remained unfinished (he died in 1813). Thus, some six score years later, Soviet composers were to start turning out operas, cantatas, symphonies, and other works of all kinds commemorating the events of the 1917 revolution and the deeds of Soviet Russia's soldiers, sailors, and airmen; and also the great events of the past.

To sum up: The early Russians were entirely dependent, in all practical respects, upon what little they were able to learn from Western example and practice. Those who impulsively wished to achieve a national style and atmosphere could do so only to a limited extent. Even if a composer of surpassing genius had been born, he could not have gone much farther in that particular direction: even in the West, technical processes had not reached a sufficient degree of diversity and flexibility.

CHAPTER IV

SPECIAL FEATURES OF RUSSIAN MUSIC

THIS is a chapter of technicalities, intended as a demonstration, in as brief and simplified a form as possible, of the effects of the pull of native and Eastern folk-music on the idiom and methods of the great nineteenth-century Russians. It may be skipped—at least at first reading—by those readers who are willing to take the matter for granted.

In all countries, without exception, folk-music and church-music are the basis of culture-music and art-forms. If we were to start seeking how much the style of Beethoven's symphonies or that of Verdi's operas owes to German and Italian folk-music respectively, we should reap almost as rich a harvest as when studying the relation of Balakiref, Borodin, or Mussorgsky's music to Russian and Eastern folk-music. But in Western Europe the art of musical composition pursued its evolution away from folk-music, following a course of its own to which we owe all the great art-forms and styles:

> Community singing produced harmony, harmony produced the major–minor key system [as opposed to the modes of church- and folk-music]: the forms of the sonata and the symphony, and the idiom of classical music, are essentially the products of this system.
>
> (H. C. Colles, *Voice and Verse*, London, 1928.)

Nothing of the kind happened in Russia. So, modern composers had to cope, on the one hand, with the desire, and indeed the necessity, to resort to art forms originating in a tradition in the establishing and maintaining of which Russia had taken no part; and, on the other hand, with the pull of the long and strong tradition of native folk- and church-music—of a music to which current structural principles bore practically no relation; of a tradition that led in a different direction, which inborn, deep-rooted impulses prompted them to follow.

In the major–minor key system of the West, tonality rests on the three harmonies of the tonic, dominant, and subdominant (that is, the first, fifth, and fourth degrees of the scale), the cadences that provide the punctuation of the musical discourse being determined thereby. In all major keys, and also in all minor, the relative

28

position in the scale of whole-tone and semi-tone intervals is the same. In modal scales, on the contrary, the relative position of those intervals varies according to the mode. Consequently, the same thing (except for key-colour) can be said in any major or in any minor key. But the same thing cannot be said in major as in minor, nor can it be said in any two of the old modes. The note-contents of every mode is identical, contrary to what happens in the major–minor keys; but the centre, the relation, and the perspective are different. The perspective, notably, depends not upon the tonic, but upon the final note of the tune, which is the rallying-point.

The modal scales of Russian folk-music differ in many respects from those of the old Greek or mediaeval modes: so much so, that certain experts prefer to describe them, not as modal, but as tonal, with certain degrees flattened or raised. This practice is misleading, because tonal scales, even after certain degrees in them are altered, continue to behave as tonal—to have, for instance, their dominant on the fifth degree, and to have as their rallying-point the tonic, not a modal final. In the scales we are now considering, the second degree often plays the part of dominant, sometimes that of subdominant; and the dominant, like the " teneure " in Gregorian chant, may be the third, fourth, or sixth degree. All this opened endless possibilities. The incorporation into modern music of the valuable idiosyncrasies of the modal scales was to prove a great gain from the point of view of technique, idiom, and structure.

> The essence of the folk-song idiom is that the melody swings boldly from pivot to pivot, and does not employ the balances of " civilized " music. . . . But it is possible to take the pivots of the folk-scale on a different plan or in a different order: to take the facts of mode and distribute them by keys, and so combine the directness of the one with the strength of the other.
>
> (A. H. Fox-Strangways in *Music and Letters*, April 1920.)

For instance, the character of the modal scales had its repercussions on harmony. These scales, to begin with, admit of a great variety of harmonic interpretations. There is no longer any need to base the harmonic scheme on the unvarying tripod tonic-dominant-subdominant, nor to bring into play, when variety and flexibility are needful, the " incongruous dainties " of excessive chromaticism.

Here is one example. There is in Mussorgsky's *Boris Godunof* (pp. 385–388 of the Russian State, Oxford University Press edition) a song whose scale is that of the Æolian mode, or mode of A, the key being F minor with flattened seventh E flat. The harmony consists, first of a chord of the major ninth on E flat, introduced gradually, note by note, with intervening passing-notes, the ground-note coming in afterwards; and finally, of the B flat minor triad, whose three notes were part of the above-mentioned ninth, and whose coming was forecast by several appearances of an A natural among the passing-notes. The effect of this simple device is tremendous (*cf.* Ex. 2 at end of book).

Modulations no longer depend exclusively upon chromatic changes cancelling tonic, dominant, and subdominant and creating a new dominant harmony and new leading-note. Indeed, most modal scales have no leading-note. The range of modulations available is considerably extended: we may have change of key only, or of mode only, or of both mode and key.

" Can it be ", a distinguished critic asked, after hearing, in 1935, the Soviet composer Shostakovitch's First Symphony, "that we are at the commencement of a new development of music that will consist not so much in destroying the old distinctions between the functions of the notes of the scale—as the atonalists would do—as in writing new meanings upon music by modifying its grammar in obedience to hereditary impulses of race and culture?" In point of fact, the commencement in question is to be traced back to Glinka, and in the music of Balakiref, Borodin, and Mussorgsky, composed in the 'sixties and 'seventies, we see the new development well under way.

Some of the new departures carry us so far off the beaten track that they raise hard problems for analysts, and especially nomenclators. The opening motif of Borodin's B minor symphony (see Ex. 3 at end of book) is a case in point. Two of its notes do not belong to the scale of B minor, and this has given rise to various comments, some of them curious. One Russian critic says that the C natural and D sharp belong to the scale of E minor, subdominant of B minor, and so do contribute to confirm the main key. Another (not Russian) declares that he cannot help hearing the motif as in E minor, the D sharp being a " real " note; and a third, that all becomes clear if we assume it to be in D major, with flattened seventh (C natural) and second (D sharp for E flat). Neither of these two explanations holds water, for the simple reason that here B un-questionably behaves as a tonic. Once this fact is accepted, three explanations are possible; and of the three, only one is reasonably simple: that the scale is B Phrygian (the key of B in the mode of E), with D sharp as a passing-note. The other two would entail references to the chromatic mode of old Greek and Byzantine music, and to the variable scales to be found in Russian folk-music.

Another, even more important point—but one with which it is impossible to deal adequately within the limits of this brief chapter—is that the " facts of the modes " had their repercussions not only on melodic and harmonic texture, but also on form.   They account for architectural features unknown to Western tradition : for instance, a piece of music ending otherwise than with a full close—maybe otherwise than on the tonic, and even on a discord, as happens with Mussorgsky, and as became current practice with Debussy and Ravel.   A corollary is that a work on a big scale may end in a key other than that of the beginning (Balakiref's *Tamara*, Rimsky-Korsakof's *Antar*) : which certainly shows the grammar of music modified with a vengeance.

The metres and rhythms of folk-music, too, play a big part in modern Russian music.   In the West, communal singing had not only produced harmony and the major–minor system, but made for simplicity and symmetry of rhythm.   The principle was unexceptionable in itself so far as it made for orderliness and shapeliness : but it again meant an impoverishment, the elimination of many valuable resources, a rigid and restrictive conception of metre and rhythm.   Rhythmic schemes came to consist exclusively of either binary or ternary units arranged in symmetrical patterns and periods, in two-bar and four-bar lengths and their multiples.   In Russian folk-song, not only quintuple and septuple time, but supple and complex combinations, such as, among many others, $\frac{5}{4} + \frac{2}{4} + \frac{2}{4} +$ $\frac{2}{4}, \frac{7}{8} + \frac{6}{8} + \frac{5}{8}$, and $\frac{6}{4} + \frac{5}{4} + \frac{3}{4}$, are common.   The Russian nationalists, being free from Western inhibitions and prejudices, were able to avail themselves of these interesting possibilities.   All this ran counter to musical tradition and usage, both of which discouraged modal leanings and irregularities of rhythm.[1]   But by the time the Russians appeared on the scene, symptoms of a tendency to extend boundaries, if not to do away with most of them altogether, were

[1] Cecil Sharp, in *English Folk-Song, Some Conclusions* (London, 1907), has pungent remarks to offer on Brahms's harmonic interpretations of modal tunes in his *Seven Books of German Folk-Songs*.   Mr. Ernest Newman has repeatedly called attention to the pull of convention upon Brahms : pointing out, for instance, that even when setting prose-texts (in *Vier Ernste Gesänge*), he compelled the prose to conform to musical patterns that were at the opposite remove from the freedom and flexibility that are the very life of prose.   These two instances are advanced here merely in order to illustrate the difference of attitude, Brahms being an uncompromising exponent of the classical tradition, including the drawbacks referred to in the first chapter of this book.

already apparent: for instance, Beethoven's beginning his first symphony out of the key, his and Schubert's bold tonal schemes, new and daring harmonic devices in Schubert's, Liszt's, Chopin's, and Schumann's music, Berlioz's asymmetric melodies, Schumann's ending a song on a chord of the dominant seventh, occasional experiments in quintuple time (Chopın, Boieldieu, Reicha, and others). But with the advent of the Russians, things started proceeding speedily: so speedily, indeed, that outside Russia Liszt was the only one capable of keeping pace with the nationalist innovators; the first, too, to understand and praise Balakiref, Borodin, and Mussorgsky.

All these innovations have long since passed into everyday practice. And some people are apt to forget the part the nationalist Russians played in introducing them and proving their artistic value: among others, the critic alluded to earlier in this chapter (p. 30), and Sir George Dyson, who in *The New Music* (London, 1924) mentions but one of them, Rimsky-Korsakof, and gives a solitary example—and not a particularly typical one—from his music. One reason for this strange and unfair oversight may be that long before becoming known in other Western countries, Russian national music left its imprint on Debussy and Ravel, from whom their contemporaries and juniors in turn learnt much that they themselves had learnt from the example set by the great Russians. Of course innovations of this kind—or indeed of any kind—should never be judged in the light of theoretical considerations, either favourable or unfavourable: it is the freedom acquired, the opening of new perspectives, that is a gain. How successfully composers avail themselves of the new opportunities is a matter that must be considered afresh in each individual case.

As shown by the verdicts (two among many) quoted at the beginning of Chapter II, p. 17, the initiative taken by the Russians was first regarded, in many quarters, as begetting ugliness, disorder, and anarchy. This is to a certain extent understandable. Their innovations came as a rude shock to habits.

A technical description (especially if it be brief and summary, as is here the case) of the Russians' processes seems to suggest lawlessness, a state of things in which everything is licit, nothing forbidden, nothing even regulated. In actual fact, they betoken not lack of discipline, but, to quote a memorable saying of Debussy's, "discipline sought in freedom, not in the formulae of an obsolete theory, good for weaklings only". The mutual impact of Western tradition and Russian elements caused the modal scales to react upon the idiom and forms begotten by the tonal principle; and these in turn to react upon the modal scales and compel them to fall into order according to a new discipline. Under such conditions, the composer is forced to create a new technique:

> Whence, Fox-Strangways remarks in the essay already mentioned, the verdicts that he "lacks technique", that his counterpoint is "untidy", that his harmonies "do not modulate"—verdicts pronounced by critics who do not understand the task he has set himself to accomplish.

Thus, too, Sir Donald Tovey, referring to "the transformation of Mussorgsky's *Boris Godunof* at the hands of Rimsky-Korsakof", describes Rimsky-Korsakof's mind as "incapable of telling a blunder from a stroke of genius or a feature of style".

The Russians did not go so far as might be regarded as theoretically possible. We could imagine, in an ideal state of things, an art of composition evolving in a hypothetical Russia, civilized yet closely in touch with its own native music; generations of composers building up, throughout centuries, on the modal principle instead of away from it, and giving us, in the course of time, forms as ripe and complex and perfect as the Western symphony and sonata, yet as different from these as, say, the Elizabethan drama is from the tragedy of Corneille and Racine. But Glinka and his successors, suddenly launched in the midst of things, had to make their own bricks (and indeed to learn the technique of brick-making), as well as to discover the structural principles of which they stood in need. Considering the formidable difficulties in their way, the wonder is, not that they should have failed to do better, but that they should have achieved as much as they did. Their music, besides constituting a link failing which the course of idiom and technique between the Berlioz–Chopin period and the Debussy–Ravel period might have been different, has proved its vitality by living. A complete study should, of course, cover its shortcomings as well as its merits. For such a purpose, Gerald Abraham's books (see Bibliography) will prove an invaluable complement to this introductory survey.

Understanding the tasks the Russians set themselves to achieve is not difficult, provided the new conditions be borne in mind. For instance, the major–minor system, which demands the affirmation of tonality by means of the tonic, dominant, and subdominant harmonies, supplies no means of finding a suitable and aesthetically satisfying harmonization of tunes such as the one referred to on p. 30 above: but the modally-minded Mussorgsky solved the problem brilliantly. It is characteristic of his partiality for radical solutions that once, Rimsky-Korsakof having described a transition he had devised in order to render less abrupt the passing from the key in which the third movement of his *Antar* ended to that of the following finale, he should have replied:

> Is it true indeed that after the pompous key of D major has been asserted, aesthetic taste calls for the note A in order to introduce the melancholic, pathetic D flat major? What could be more poetic, after the *forte* in D major, than the wistful D flat major straightforth, without any preparation?

The consequences of " taking the facts of modes and distributing them by keys " may be unexpected. They may include, as already mentioned, dispensing with a return to the main key at the end of a composition. Balakiref's wonderful tone-poem *Tamara* has an opening section in B minor; the sequel is mainly in D flat major. At the end, the music of the opening section reappears in that key. Instead of first hearing a key that will finally assert its ascendancy over materials introduced later in another key (which is the basic feature of classical form), we begin by hearing materials over which a key introduced later will finally assert its ascendancy. This is a perfectly logical plan. It is, in fact, an extension of the modal principle, according to which the rallying point is the final, not the tonic, as in the major–minor system. Critics who aver that failure to return to the main key betokens ignorance or carelessness will do well to note, in the last quarter or so of *Tamara*, the many points at which the music passes from D flat major to B minor or conversely, so that nothing could have been easier than to make it end in B minor had Balakiref elected to do so. But then, it will be felt, the perspective would have been different—far less imaginative and significant.

Obviously, the waiving of the old rule is neither good nor bad in itself. It would be inconceivable with regard to sonata form, of which this rule is the very basis. But as soon as we admit that sonata form is not the *ne plus ultra* of musical art (and the whole history of music during the past century compels us to admit it), we see that it is all to the good that composers should be able to ignore the pull of convention in the matter of form as well as in that of harmony, rhythm, and melodic design.

The procedure, of course, must be justified by the event. Mussorgsky's songs provide many examples of splendid results achieved by breaking the old rule. In *Serenade* (in the set *Songs and Dances of Death*) we have a first section in an elusive E minor; the second part, which brings a complete change of atmosphere—Death's despotic wooing, in answer to a maiden's vague, languid dreams—⬩ is in E flat minor, firmly asserted.   In the same set, *Lullaby*, evoking a dialogue between Death and a mother imploring him to spare her child, is in F sharp minor with many alterations, but ends abruptly on a cadence to A minor, with Death's utterance: " See, my song has lulled him to sleep . . . sleep, baby, sleep. . . ."

Should it be objected that what may be tolerated in a song, on the strength of the words, remains inexpedient in instrumental music, the case of *Tamara* provides a conclusive reply.   Many theorists dismiss structures of this order as merely rhapsodic. Granting for the sake of argument that the label may be technically correct, we need not grant that it implies inferiority.

On the subject of rhapsodic methods in melody-building, Dyson, in *The New Music*, offers relevant remarks that can be extended to cover the whole field:

> The formal element in melody is no standard of its worth. What may safely be said is that the power to write convincing rhapsody is a rare gift.   Let there be the smallest failure of inspiration, and the composer is meandering.   It is a most exacting form of art, in which genius must never be intermittent.   Our contemporaries who rhapsodize must be given the credit of accepting formidable risks.

And, on the subject of form, he points out that there are two essential factors: the factor of economy, which means the fitting use of material; and the factor of coherence, which means coherence of style, which relates the details of a work to the whole of it, and does not permit incongruous aberrations of fancy.   These terms, he adds, are not in any sense technical definitions, but represent sufficiently definite reactions to experience to be capable of a broad application to values of all kinds.

CHAPTER V

GLINKA, DARGOMYJSKY, SEROF

WITH Glinka we are no longer, as we were even with his immediate predecessors, on the fringe of national Russian music: the best he has given us carries us right *in medias res*. He was the first Russian composer of genius, and the first in whose music we observe the effects of that pull of native and Eastern folk-music which was briefly described in the foregoing chapter. He was an intuitive creator first and last, not a theorist or a system-monger who set out to innovate or reform. As already stated, he merely wished " to compose music in which his beloved fellow-countrymen would feel quite at home, and not to strut about in borrowed plumes ".

He felt that in order to do so, he would have to steer clear of a good many conventions and current habits. " I could never sincerely become an Italian in music," he wrote when studying in Italy. Later, he discarded a tone-poem he was composing because " he found it impossible to get out of the German rut as regarded working-out ". The problems set by the modal folk-tune elements he felt compelled to use were novel, and he had no precedent to guide him. At twenty-two he composed a cantata that was partly in C major and partly in B flat major—an unusual and ticklish plan, obviously dictated by the pull of his inborn modal instinct (see above, p. 29). He confesses, in his *Memoirs*, that " he did not succeed in co-ordinating those two keys quite successfully ". Even in *A Life for the Tsar*, on which he started work in 1835, at the age of thirty-one, he often—but not always—went astray when venturing into modal regions. Yet he achieved more than enough to stir his audiences to enthusiasm, and make them feel that the music spoke in truly Russian accents, in accents never heard before in a musical composition.

The feeling persists to the present day. It is difficult for non-Russians to share it, and even to realize why it should have persisted. In 1836 *A Life for the Tsar* was, in many respects, far more Russian than anything ever heard before. In the light of later developments, beginning with the works of Glinka's maturity, and above all *Ruslan and Liudmila*, it is, as an example of national style, very tentative and restricted in scope, except for a few strokes of genius such as a lovely, strikingly vernacular little bridal chorus in Act III. Apart from that, there is much in it that is well thought out, well carried out, and effective.

Ruslan and Liudmila, first performed six years later (1842), is uneven too, but contains much that is of rare originality and beauty. The choral parts in the first act, in archaic, truly Russian style, the Persian maidens' chorus in the second, the fantastic scenes and fairy music in the second and fourth, the Eastern dances in the fourth, and a good many of the songs, show far-reaching vision and full power to achieve. It is deplorable that all this lovely music should remain unknown outside its country of origin. Elsewhere, music-lovers have practically no chance of getting acquainted with it.

Neither *A Life for the Tsar* nor *Ruslan* is likely to gain a footing on opera-stages abroad. They contain too much that would prove tedious to all but confirmed devotees of old-fashioned, full-dress grand opera, even though the former has at least the advantage of a well-knit and, although slow-moving, really dramatic plot. But of *Ruslan*, whose libretto is disastrously feeble and incoherent, most of the finest portions, instrumental and vocal, would lend themselves admirably to concert and broadcast performance. It is a mystery why only the Overture should have found its way into the concert repertory: even the Eastern dances (and especially the magnificent *Lesghinka*, an outstanding example of Glinka's genius as an orches- trator) remaining neglected.

Of his other representative works, only one, the orchestral *Kamarinskaya*, is played fairly often. The others are *Jotà Aragonesa* and *Summer Night in Madrid* for orchestra, and the *Prince Kholmsky* incidental music. These half-dozen works exercised a decisive influence on Glinka's successors. They are the fountain-head of Russian national music, almost every characteristic aspect of which appears in them.

The first two composers who came after Glinka were Dargo- myjsky (1813–1869) and Serof (1820–1871). Both devoted them- selves chiefly to dramatic music. Both, especially Dargomyjsky, have their importance from the historian's point of view: but the fact that nothing of the latter's output, and very little of the former's, have endured does not, like the neglect of Glinka's music, spell a great loss to music-lovers.

Neither was gifted with creative genius. Serof's music is un- original, shallow, motley in style. Dargomyjsky evolved a con- ception of realism in opera, and especially in dramatic recitative, which had much in common with older conceptions, from Caccini's and Monteverdi's to Gluck's. But the one opera in which he carried it into practice, *The Stone Guest* (1869), is a dry-as-dust, lifeless affair except for a few striking details. He had a certain sense of characterization, but no lyrical imagination or feeling, and he commanded but very few resources. In some of his songs and in his orchestral *Kazatchok*, *Baba-Yaga* (The Witch), and *Fantasy on Finnish Themes*, he struck a new vein here and there, but did not go very far. His high aims and conscientious experiments proved stimulating to his juniors, and especially to Mussorgsky on the threshold of his artistic maturity. He foresaw the possibilities of a new genre, which came to its own a little later with Rimsky-Korsakof and Mussorgsky: the opera of manners, in which evocations of native types and of the life and ways of the people would play a big part—a part often more important than the dramatic action and psychological under-currents. He tried to carry it into execution in his *Russalka* (1856), and achieved a measure of success in the comedy scenes.

The same may be said of Serof, on the strength of the evocations of pagan Russia in his opera *Rogneda* (1865), and of the carnival scenes in *The Power of Evil*—among the first of the crowd scenes that are a remarkable feature in many Russian operas.

It is sometimes alleged that his operas influenced Mussorgsky. There is a measure of truth in the allegation: but while suggesting to him things worth doing, they showed him clearly how not to do them, as can be seen from a letter of his to Balakiref on the opera *Judith* (1863). Unfortunately there is no room to quote and discuss here this most instructive document.

CHAPTER VI

BALAKIREF, CUI, BORODIN

THE first to carry on from the point reached by Glinka was Mili Balakiref (1837–1910). Glinka, except for his orchestral fantasies, had done little or nothing in any field but that of dramatic music. With Balakiref, the national style manifests itself for the first time in the bigger forms of symphonic music, in song, and in piano music. Balakiref's style, like Glinka's at its most original and ripest, is rooted in traditional music, Russian and Eastern. Its melodic character, its rhythms, its harmonic texture, its colours are thereby determined. He uses actual folk-tunes freely; and even when he does not, the modal and other idiosyncrasies of folk-music affect his invention and procedure—for instance, in *Tamara* (see Chapter IV, p. 34). Now, this is the kind of thing on which most of the onslaughts against vernacular national music are based, the practice of using traditional elements either as actual materials in composition or as models for invented materials being condemned as the last resource of composers who have no capacity for real invention, as a makeshift, and moreover as unprofitable for the alleged reason that folk-tunes (and, it would seem, not only lyrical song-tunes, but even dance-tunes or any other kind of tune) do not lend themselves to symphonic treatment—an unwise generalization; Glazunof's *Stenka Razin* (see Chapter XI, p. 75) and d'Indy's *Symphonie Montagnarde* afford superb examples of folk-tunes symphonically treated.

One well-known English scholar wound up a wholesale disquisition against the practice with the assertion that " the more elements borrowed from folk-music appear in a work, the less himself the composer is ". This, if it were true, would make it easy to demonstrate the degree of originality that composers display when using folk-tunes by means of an arithmetical operation as elementary as that by which Alice showed Humpty-Dumpty how many days there are in the year when you can receive " unbirthday " presents (contents of the work, 365; borrowed from folk music, 1; remains composer's contribution, 364). But, in actual fact, things are not so simple.

Can it be seriously asserted that themes invented under the influence of folk-music (or of church-music, an equally important factor) are necessarily more derivative than themes invented under

the influence of the thousand and one elements that go to the formation of every composer's mind and craftsmanship? It stands to
reason that whether a composer acquires his schooling by the study
of other compositions exclusively, or whether he turns his attention
to folk-music and church-music, he can be equally original or
equally lacking in originality.

As regards the borrowing of actual folk-tunes, no better justifica-
tion of the practice need be sought than that afforded by Balakiref's
piano fantasy *Islamey* (1863). This is built on three very simple
themes, the first two Caucasian dance-tunes, mainly rhythmical,
the third an Armenian song, an organized melody, expressive and
attractive, but not particularly significant in itself. To ask whether
he could or should have invented themes equal in value, potential
or actual, to these instead of borrowing would be merely childish.
The important point is that he saw in those unassuming elements
potentialities which no one else could have seen, let alone turn to
account. And from them he derived a wonderful pageantry of
rioting sounds and colours, an extraordinarily telling evocation,
stamped throughout with his strongly marked, highly distinctive
personality, of Eastern sunshine and shimmer and languor and
turmoil.

Another case in point is his superb tone-poem *Russia* (1861,
published in revised form in 1904), composed for the commemora-
tion of the thousandth anniversary of the foundation of the Russian
State. It is built on three folk-tunes, selected so that their musical
character should be suitable to symbolize, the composer explained,
the three principal aspects of Russia's history: pagan Russia, the
Muscovite State, and the quasi-democratic old Russia.

It is impressively beautiful, and constitutes a perfect example of
thorough fusion of the materials into a whole that is a highly
individual artistic achievement. And further confirmation is to be
found in the finale of his C major symphony, whose main subject is
the tune of a bouncing Russian patter-song, an Eastern dance-
tune providing a contrasting subject.

Other works testify to his fondness for using folk-tunes: his
early overture on a Spanish theme communicated to him by Glinka;
a prelude in his incidental music to *King Lear* (1861, published in
1904 only) consisting of delightful variations on an old English
tune; and the tone-poem *In Bohemia* (1867, published in revised
form in 1906), a pendant to his *Russia*, composed, he said,

> in the hope that it would help to foster interest in the native
> music of that lovable little nation, which so sturdily resisted
> Germany's attempts to absorb it.

But in his greatest masterpiece, *Tamara* (begun in the 'sixties, finished in 1882), there are no borrowings from folk-music except a dance-tune or two. *Tamara* is a tone-poem inspired by Lermontof's poem about a wanton Caucasian queen, who lured passers-by into her mountain castle: that is, by a circumstantial programme. There was a time when purists would denounce programme-music as a sin, against the alleged spirit of the art, very much as happened later with regard to borrowings from folk-music. Fortunately, it is no longer needful to confute that assertion, it having become clear enough by now that it is the achievement, not the starting-point, that matters; and that music, whatever its source of inspiration and aims may be, is to be judged as music pure and simple.

Tone-poems of this kind form an important part of the national Russian repertory; and among them, *Tamara* [1] stands unparalleled for its poetic beauty and significance from the purely musical point of view. As mentioned in Chapter I, most of the Russian tone-poems are based on concrete, unambitious subjects, free from abstract philosophical or symbolic connotations. One may ask whether this did not unavoidably make for music which, whatever its other merits might be, was bound to remain deficient in that deep-rooted relationship to human life that we find in the greatest masterpieces. *Tamara* enables us to settle the question. On the surface it may be a musical version of the story of a wanton with a habit of murdering her lovers. But it has deep under-currents. And from the mystery-laden introduction, evoking the weird, spacious landscape, to the climax and conclusion, of truly Lucretian grandeur (it might have been inspired by the Latin poet's famous lines that describe " welling from the very fount of delight, the waters of bitterness and disenchantment "), the appeal to the imagination, the human significance, is direct and potent.

Even the finest of Balakiref's orchestral works (including his second symphony, finished in 1908) are sadly neglected. Stranger still, even the most beautiful of his songs and piano pieces, which ought long since to have been given the place they deserve in the home and concert repertory, remain very little known. He was the first Russian to compose songs that rise to as high a level as Schubert's and Schumann's: especially among those he turned out in the late 'fifties and early 'sixties, the *Song of the Golden Fish* mentioned in Chapter I, the *Hebraic Song*, and above all the *Song of Georgia*, wonderfully poetic and moving; and, in a set of ten that appeared

[1] The ballet *Tamara*, first produced in 1913 by the Diaghilef company, may pass muster as a matter-of-fact, pedestrian choreographic interpretation of the story, but its character bears no relation whatever to that of Balakiref's music, ill-advisedly used for it.

in 1904, *Prelude*, a poignant evocation of the tragedy that was ever Russia's; *Vision*, of epic grandeur, a dream-picture of Easter Day in Prague, with hymns rising and bells ringing; *Vernal Night*, a lovely little idyll in which he ventured, unexpectedly, into the realm of the new musical impressionism for which he had but little liking : a *Lullaby*, with a fairly long instrumental introduction, the stanzas contrasting, in far-reaching, haunting accents, the sleep of the child, the man, and the ancient; and another song on a big scale, a setting of a poem by Khomiakof describing the opening of Napoleon's tomb at St. Helena—a notable item in the catalogue of music (nearly all of it Russian) about Napoleon. Another set of ten, published in the 'nineties, contains, among other interesting things, a jolly, almost Mussorgsky-ish little tippler's song, the one example of humorous characterization to be found in his output.

Cesar Cùi (1835–1918) is generally mentioned as the leader, jointly with Balakiref, of the national movement. His father was French, his mother Lithuanian. Whether she had any Russian forbears is not known. Anyhow, there can have been but little Russian blood in him; and this may help to account for the fact that his music is, in feeling and character, not in the least Russian. Even though he eagerly championed, in countless articles, pamphlets, and books, the cause of the Russian national group as he saw it, his own compositions can hardly be regarded as coming anywhere near the standard he wished to achieve.

The non-vernacular character of his music is, in itself, of no importance. The point is that it has no distinctive character whatsoever. His style is reminiscent of Auber's, of Schumann's, and here and there of Dargomyjsky's; and he never succeeded in acquiring sufficient technical ability. His deficiencies, however, were compensated in a measure by his feeling for lyrical melody and his sense of grace and delicacy. So, whereas none of his major works—half a dozen operas and four orchestral suites among others—has endured, his songs (about two hundred in number), his piano pieces, and other compositions on a small scale have won him a place among the minor poets of music.

The legend of the nationalist group, nicknamed "the mighty handful" in Russia, and pompously described, elsewhere, as "The Great Five" (its other members Borodin, Mussorgsky, and Rimsky-Korsakof, all three pupils of Balakiref), has given rise to much empty talk *pro et contra*, and to many ridiculous misconceptions. In France, at one time, excitable and irresponsible apologists were wont to descant upon the "collective personality" of the members of the group, as if such a thing could ever exist in art. Of course, the only things common to the " Five " (or rather, to four of them, Cui, as just mentioned, having to be left out of count), and to later comers such as Liadof, Glazunof, Liapunof, and a good many others, were certain idiosyncrasies of idiom, style, and procedure, all of which are to be traced back to Glinka.

Balakiref's teaching did much to expand and instil Glinka's methods; so did his own works, especially in the early days. In fact, Glinka and he had struck the only line along which the new national music could develop. His own innovations, like Glinka's, soon became current usage. To avail oneself of them did not entail sacrificing any measure of one's independence and inborn originality.

Alexander Borodin (1833–1887), for instance, is, as much as Balakiref, in direct line of succession to Glinka; and he also owes much to Balakiref. He is a strong, distinctive, lovable personality, robust and genial, virile and sensitive. His output is small, but all of it is significant and thoroughly satisfying.

His two symphonies and two string quartets—but especially the second symphony (1876) and the first quartet (1877)—are in a class by themselves. All his gifts—his capacity for melodic, harmonic, and rhythmic invention, his sense of colour and form—appear in them at their best. The structure is firm and logical, however unconventional it may be from the point of view of stereotyped theory: " his musical organisms grow and live, and shape themselves in growing " (G. Abraham). He is a bold innovator in the province of harmony, the boldest of the nineteenth-century Russians after Mussorgsky; and his innovations, like Mussorgsky's, have permanently enriched the vocabulary of music. For instance, he was the first to feel how valuable for expressive purposes in moods of softness and charm certain so-called sharp discords, such as consecutive seconds, could be. He achieved, notably in his songs *The Queen of the Sea* and *The Enchanted Garden*, truly lovely effects by means of them, effects of the same kind as those that play a big part in Debussy's and Ravel's music. But in his day, that kind of thing was regarded as intolerable and abominable. Certain critics availed themselves of the fact that one of his songs was entitled *The False Note*, and another *My Song is Fierce and Bitter*, to deride him; and he was freely described as " an arch-enemy of music ". Meanwhile, Liszt was urging him to listen to nobody and to forge ahead unperturbed: " you go far, but never astray. You are on the right track, and may safely trust your intuition."

Liszt was right. Borodin's intuition served him admirably. His assets included rare clarity of vision and sureness of touch. No better proof need be sought than his orchestral tone-picture, *In the*

44   A SURVEY OF RUSSIAN MUSIC

Steppes of Central Asia (1880). It required an unusually high quality of imagination to make of this simple sketch (a trifle, intended merely to provide a background to a *tableau vivant* showing a caravan crossing the steppe under the protection of Russian soldiers) the lovely, thoroughly self-sufficient, and highly suggestive little gem of pure music it is.

These gifts are manifest even in his first symphony (begun 1862, finished 1867), the earliest of his big works. It reveals a measure of inexperience in the art of conceiving and selecting, but not so in the execution. The second (1877) is masterly throughout. Weingartner, half a century ago, declared that it was one of the most important of the post-Beethoven period; and the best critics of many countries have endorsed this judgment. Most of this symphony is epic in style and character. Borodin, like Glinka, was most at ease and most thoroughly himself in epic, or in purely lyrical moods. It is by virtue of the wealth of beautiful epic-heroic and lyrical music it contains that his one opera, *Prince Igor*, which he began in 1869, but left not quite finished (it was ably completed by Rimsky-Korsakof and Glazunof), lives. It is devoid of dramatic interest, and the libretto (his own work) is so loosely put together as to be meaningless. Still, parts of it provided a fertile field for his creative imagination—plenty of opportunities for lyricism, wistful and exalted in turn, for vehement heroic accents, poetry and passion, delicate tints, and flaming colours, picturesque vernacular and archaic grandeur, in arias and cantilenas, choruses and instrumental episodes. The wonderful Polovtsian Dances are among the greatest things in the score.

There are comic scenes, too (between two jesters, introduced into the libretto for no other purpose than to provide these scenes), revealing an entirely different side of Borodin's nature. He stands unique among the Russians of his time for his sense of musical humour and farce: nothing like Mussorgsky's realistically purposeful comic sense, but genial, fanciful pleasantry, informed by sheer animal spirits. We also see it displayed in one or two of his songs, in the part-song *Serenade of Four Swains to a Lady*, and in his contributions to the collective *Paraphrases on the Theme of the Chopsticks Polka* for piano duet,[1] in which he combines with the *Chopsticks* ostinato the earnest, tragic strains of a Funeral March and a Requiem.

In 1867 he turned out a farcical opera in five acts, *The Bogatyrs* (*The Valiant Knights*), which contained, apart from parodies of music by Meyerbeer, Rossini, Serof, and others, a good deal of

[1] The other contributors were Cui, Rimsky-Korsakof, and Liadof.

original music, said to be very bright and witty. This was produced at Moscow, but never published. The revival in 1936 will be
alluded to in Chapter XIV.

His instrumental scherzi—the principal are those in the first
quartet, the second symphony, the third (unfinished) symphony,[1]
and one in A flat major that he composed in 1880 in two versions,
for piano and for orchestra—are amazingly original, sparkling, and
exhilarating. The moods they embody range from the wistful,
nonchalant dreaminess of the one in A flat to the poetic, elfin
whimsicality of the one in the quartet—an outstanding example of
Borodin's ingenuity in the matter of instrumental writing—and the
irrepressible mirth of the one in the second symphony.

Such is the personality revealed in his music. That his output
should have been so small is ever to be regretted, considering the
value of what he achieved: " no musician has ever claimed immor-
tality with so slender an offering; yet, if there be, indeed, immortali-
ties in music, his claim is incontestable " (H. Hadow, in *Collected
Essays*).

Maybe his orchestral works, few as they are, give us all that he
was intended by nature to give in that province, even though he was
a splendid manipulator of the orchestra. He had no great inclination for the piano: a charming *Petite Suite*, consisting of seven
simple pieces, is his only contribution to its repertory, apart from
the few already mentioned. His long struggle with *Igor* may be
regarded as proving that he was not cut out for opera. But of
light, humorous, and comic music, songs, and chamber-music he
might well, had he been able to devote himself wholly to composition, have given us far more than he did. No other member of the
group had a bent for chamber-music: not even Balakiref, although
he was a keen student of Beethoven's quartets. Mussorgsky never
was really inclined towards instrumental composition. Rimsky-
Korsakof wrote, in his early days, one published string quartet
and one sextet, mainly by way of exercise. And Borodin records
that Mussorgsky and Vladimir Stassof (the mentor of the group),
when they heard that he was engaged in composing a string quartet,
were greatly distressed—a curious attitude, for which neither
Stassof's writings, nor Mussorgsky's, provide any explanation.
But to him it was an eminently suitable medium, one that he had
instinctively selected for his first youthful ventures, at a time when
he had not yet begun to learn the craft of composition. His mature
output includes, besides two string quartets, only the scherzo in

---

[1] The two movements of it that are published were completed by
Glazunof and Rimsky-Korsakof.

Les Vendredis and an exqusite *Serenata alla Spagnola* in another collective work, the *Quartet on the name B-la-F* (see p. 80); but that little is enough to put him in the front rank—the first quartet especially: it is one of the finest things in modern chamber-music.

Of the songs, thirteen in number, a few are of no great importance. But *The Sleeping Princess, The Queen of the Sea, The False Note, My Song is Fierce and Bitter, The Song of the Dark Forest,* and *The Enchanted Garden* rise to a very high level. The romantic ballad *The Sea* is very effective.

CHAPTER VII

MUSSORGSKY

MUSSORGSKY, too, has given us examples of the national Russian style in the Glinka–Balakiref tradition. But he also evolved, for the furtherance of special expressive and evocative purposes, an amazingly bold and pregnant idiom, many features of which were utterly novel.

In the early years of his career, he did not seem to have been destined by nature to become a revolutionary innovator. Borodin has described him, at the age of seventeen, a dapper, aristocratic little officer, rather affected and foppish, who would sit at the piano, and coquettishly waving his hands, play excerpts from *La Traviata* or *Il Trovatore*, the enraptured audience around him murmuring: "Charmant! Délicieux!" the while. That very year 1857, it is true, he had composed a lovely little song, *Little Star, Where Art Thou?*, not amateurish in the least, decidedly modal and vernacular in character. A few months later, however, he re-modelled it; and this second version (which he orchestrated) is far less interesting and original. The compositions he turned out during the next few years vary greatly not only in quality, but in kind, some of them being trite, others testifying to rare qualities of imagination.

At nineteen, he decided to devote himself entirely to music. He did not find his true path easily. In 1862 he wrote to Balakiref, from whom he had already been receiving lessons for nearly five years: "I have no particular confidence in my talent, nor do I misdoubt it. I am still seeking for a line in which I can do useful work." Soon afterwards, however, he was progressing speedily towards a goal which did not reveal itself to him until years later. Whence did the revelation come to him? In his autobiography (a sketchy, not altogether reliable document) he says that intimacy not only with Balakiref, Cui, and the critic Stassof, but also with "a wide circle of scholars and writers, such as Lamansky, Turghenief, Kostomarof, Grigorovitch, Kavelin, Pissemsky, Shevchenko, and others, greatly stimulated my mind and gave it an earnest, strictly scientific turn". Later he was to proclaim that he found intellectual intercourse with writers and painters far more instructive and stimulating than intercourse with his brother musicians.

And, in effect, it is far easier to trace his procedure back to the

47

influence of the writers he mentions than to that of any composer—including even Dargomyjsky. Grigorovitch, Turghenief, Pissemsky, were among the first Russians to introduce simple people in fiction, describing them with warm sympathy and understanding: Lamansky, a lecturer on the history of Russia, was a keen believer in nationalism, and a student of folk-lore. Kostomarof, the historian, strove above all " to give the first place in history to the life of the people in all its typical aspects ". Kavelin steadfastly proclaimed the value of empirical methods in psychology. To make a long story short, the history of Russian thought and literature at the period is that of a steady growth of interest in the people, and also in true-to-life, realistic methods in art.

From the middle 'sixties onwards, Mussorgsky was to proclaim many a time his realistic ambitions. " What I seek is life, wherever it is to be found; and truth, point-blank truth, however pungent " (to Stassof, 1875). " Art is not an end in itself, but a means of conversing with one's fellow-creatures " (*Autobiography*). And it has generally been assumed that these ambitions suffice to account for the idiosyncrasies of his musical idiom and style. This convenient explanation is not very helpful really: the term " realism " has so many meanings that, when all is said and done, it has no definite meaning whatsoever.

According to the *Encyclopædia Britannica*, realism, in art, is opposed to idealism in various senses. The realist is he who prefers to describe ugly things and to bring out unpleasant details (a thoroughly absurd definition, as will presently appear); or he who deals with individuals rather than types; or he who goes in for matter-of-fact, everyday subjects instead of more stimulating and poetic ones; or he who tries to show facts and express feelings exactly as they are without romantic distortions, exaggeration, or embellishment of any kind. This last is the least inadequate of all usual definitions.

But, so far as it means a desire to keep close to reality of feeling and straightforward, specific expression, the notion of realism in music is as old as opera. It is even older. Many mediaeval composers had tried to capture characteristic attitudes, gestures, and intonations, and to find suitable translations of them in terms of music. This ambition governed the experiments of the Florentine artists who created, in the early seventeenth century, the *stilo recitativo*. In Galileo's *Dialogues on Music Ancient and Modern* (1602), in Caccini's *Nuove Musiche* (1601), Monteverdi's letters and prefaces, and later in the writings of Lulli, Rameau, and Gluck, ideas very similar to Dargomyjsky's and Mussorgsky's are expressed, often in the very same words.

And if, as all these composers (and with them many others in various walks of art or of criticism) assert, realism consists in representing facts and expressing feelings as they really are, realism will no more lay stress upon unpleasant, ugly details than upon any others. It will treat them all alike, selecting those that are significant regardless of their pleasantness or unpleasantness. And so, realism is also opposed to formalism (which implies elaboration for the sake of reduction to order, to formal beauty as usually understood) and to romanticism, understood as implying senti-mental or melodramatic amplification.

Amplifying and formalizing methods remain very much the same whether they are applied to the ugly or the beautiful, the common-place or the egregious. An artist may select any subject under the sun, have a thoroughly realistic vision of that subject, and yet fail to give us a realistic equivalent of it—because he deals with it con-ventionally, perhaps, or because he over-stresses points, or puts too many comments of his own in his interpretation of it.

The realist, then, does not try to embellish his subject or his subject-matter by stylizing it. He aims at a maximum of veracity and specific characterization coupled with a minimum of stylization. He does not dwell upon the emotions that his subject stirs in him: he places in the foreground this subject itself (that is, the cause of his artistic emotion), and trusts that this will be the surest way of stirring up emotions of the right kind. In short, realism is a matter not of subject, but of treatment; not of emotions conveyed, but of ways of conveying them. And this, in turn, means that the principle may lead anywhere, and leads nowhere in particular. It is positive in what it prohibits rather than in what it prescribes; and is worth exactly what the artist's practical application of it is worth—neither more nor less. There is negative realism, which consists in avoiding all that might be anti-realistic: airs and graces, flowers of rhetoric, amplification, over-emphasis, and so on. And there is positive realism, which consists in using striking processes of specific, straightforward expression or evocation.

The latter is entirely a matter of creative imagination—of inspira-tion, apart from any question of method. Dargomyjsky's musical imagination being neither strong nor far-reaching, his realism remained chiefly negative. Mussorgsky was endowed with the right kind of imagination, and so achieved valuable positive results.

In short, realism is a guiding, but not an actually fecundating principle; nor could it in any circumstances determine the positive idiosyncrasies of any composer, be the composer Monteverdi, Gluck, or Mussorgsky. Nor could, of course, the philosophical and aesthetic ideas Mussorgsky absorbed do more than compel him to come to grips with his problem and work out his own solution of it by inquiring more and more searchingly into the properties of the elements he used, and into the adequacy of his methods of using them.

Only a very few of the results can be mentioned here. In his vocal parts, he was careful to keep close to the natural pace, prosody, and inflexions of speech, especially in the works of his maturity. He seldom resorted to big leaps or to strong contrasts in note-values. Intervals bigger than a sixth are uncommon. As a rule, the work is done by note-values ranging from the dotted crotchet to the semi-quaver. The same is true of his instrumental motifs.

Within these limitations, he achieves a surprising wealth of contrasts and shades, thanks to the variety of modes and harmonic schemes he resorts to. He had a keen feeling for the value of chords *per se*, single or in groups, as independent, self-sufficient units, and not as pawns in a tonal or modal scheme. He used them without the usual precautions—preparations, resolutions, gradual transitions, and so on. Of harmonic artifices, he preferred the simplest, such as passing-notes and pedal-points. He had little use for suspensions and anticipations.

All this is thoroughly in keeping with his realistic aims. Changes of rhythm and time-signature, to which he resorted very freely, may make for accuracy and pregnancy of utterance, whereas too many contrasts of note-values may introduce touches of mere grandiloquence. Bold harmonic concatenations and abrupt modulations, aptly used, are eminently suitable for effects of strong, sharp emphasis, but over-elaboration seldom is. Suspensions and anticipations may easily become ostentatious, over-pathetic. When Mussorgsky requires an emphatic or pathetic accent, he prefers to use the appoggiatura, a terser and less oratorical device; and, even so, he inclines to entrust it to the instrumental accompaniment, giving the voice a real harmonic note, and as often as not a repetition of the foregoing note rather than a rise or a fall.

Except when writing purely lyrical music, he seldom introduces amplifications or deviations for purely musical purposes. He never gives a thought to conventional rounding-off or transitions. He will pass from the F sharp major triad to the C major triad (*Boris Godunof*, Lamm edition, p. 137), modulate to G major only to break out in F sharp (*ib.*, pp. 218–219), end an Act of *Khovanshchina* (the first) or a song (*The Harper's Song*) on a discord, or give us two-part writing teeming with unisons, seconds, fourths, fifths, sevenths, and ninths (*Boris*, p. 394; see Example 5). For a few of these highly unconventional processes, precedents are to be found in

Berlioz, Schumann, Liszt, and here and there in Dargomyjsky. But there they are isolated, exceptional ventures, not style features. The real precedents are to be sought in a little-known province of Russian folk-music.

The collections of folk-songs published by Balakiref, Rimsky-Korsakof, and most others give the impression that these songs are all monodic. Most of their idiosyncrasies are inherent in their melody: notably, the modal character, naturally implying certain harmonies rather than certain others. But a good deal of the peasants' singing is part-singing—part-singing of a rough, very archaic kind, generating unexpected harmonies and abrupt, elliptic concatenations. The outcome often is widely different from anything a trained composer would have dreamt of perpetrating in those days (see Example 4).

The first to collect part-songs of that kind was Melgunof, who published a set of them in 1879. To Mussorgsky, who spent his early years in the heart of his native countryside, and later never missed an opportunity of revisiting it, this order of folk-song may have meant far more than it did to the other Russian composers; and it may well have played a part in forming his musical language.

It is true that no less an expert than Kastalsky says (in his booklet *Peculiarities of Russian Folk Music*, 1923) that of all nineteenth-century Russian music, only a single chorus—one in Borodin's *Prince Igor*—comes close to peasant part-singing. No doubt this is correct from the textual point of view: but in spirit Mussorgsky's procedure comes very close to that of the peasants.

The analogy was undoubtedly felt by Rimsky-Korsakof, who in a chapter of his autobiography applies the self-same epithet, " barbarous ", to Melgunof's notations and to music by Mussorgsky. Mussorgsky, indeed, was regarded as a barbarian by most of his fellow-composers and by the greater part of the musical public. His music came as too rude a shock to usage and habits. In the course of time, it exercised a tremendous influence on French music —especially on Debussy and Ravel, and through them, soon afterwards, the world over. In fact less than two-score years after the upheaval caused by *Boris Godunof* all his revolutionary innovations had become part and parcel of everyday practice; and nowadays, it is difficult to realize how scandalous they seemed at the time.

The story of the posthumous fate of his works will be told presently. Meanwhile, let it be stated that some of them appeared during his lifetime under his own control; but further editions of them, and all those that appeared after his death only, were more or less drastically revised and reduced to conventional order by

Rimsky-Korsakof. The reviser's sins, great in themselves, have been of late years exaggerated by zealous champions, who proclaim that whatever he touched he disfigured. Now that a critical edition of the complete works has been provided by the Russian State Publishing Department, there is no excuse for continuing to accept and propagate debased or dubious revisions; and it is easy to determine which of the other texts in circulation should be avoided.

Mussorgsky's output consists mainly of songs and dramatic music. Of his few instrumental works, the tone-poem *St. John's Night on the Bare Mountain*, the subject of which is a witches' sabbath, and the set of piano pieces *Pictures from an Exhibition*, are the most important. The *Pictures* are unequal in quality, but most of them are attractive, and testify to his rare capacity for graphic evocation.

The *Night on the Bare Mountain* exists in two genuine versions: the first orchestral, the second with chorus—both of them spirited, picturesque, high-coloured music, especially so the choral version, which Mussorgsky intended to use in his opera *The Sorotchintsy Fair* (see Chapter VIII).

The songs fall into several distinct groups or categories. Many are portrayals, pathetic or humorous, of human beings, mostly peasants or other humble creatures: a peasant woman, hopelessly bowed under the yoke of fate, rocking her baby to sleep, and foreseeing for him nothing but hard toil and gloom (*The Peasant's Lullaby*); another, who, on the contrary, foresees a better future for her infant son (*Yeremushka*); a loafer in rags, carefree, and quite philosophical as he remembers his mother's forecasts of ease and happiness (*Kallistrat*); a village simpleton, shyly singing his love for a girl who, he feels, will never respond (*Savishna*); a rascally urchin baiting an old crone (*The Street Arab*); a beggar tormented by cold and hunger (*The Orphan*); a passionate woman who voices her hatred for her old husband and dreams of her lover (*Gathering Mushrooms*); another, full-blooded and defiant, who recklessly enjoys herself while she may, thinking with contempt of her husband toiling the while (*Hopak*); children chatting, playing, day-dreaming (*The Nursery*, a set of most delightful miniature masterpieces).

In all these Mussorgsky's realism is to be seen at its fullest and truest. He gives us not mere types, but live individuals, soberly and strongly limned. The music evokes not only their feelings, but their very aspect, attitudes, and movements: "a few notes", Maria Olenin remarks in her book *Le Legs de Moussorgsky*, "and they spring up, stand before us, and lay bare their very souls before fading away into the nothingness out of which the composer had conjured them up."

Of the lyrical songs, some are mediocre, but others rise to a high level of originality and beauty: the set *Sunless*, especially, the last two of which, a cryptic, listless *Elegy* and *On the River*, loftily contemplative and serene, open wide vistas to the imagination. *Epitaph*, his tribute to the memory of his dear friend Nadejda Opotchinina, is in the same style and spirit, but free from any cryptic element. *The Jewish Song* is a lovely example of impassioned, restrained lyricism.

The humorous songs range from the light-hearted badinage of *The Garden by the Don* and *The Magpie* to the broad comedy of *The Seminarist* (a young student mingling his amorous preoccupations with the Latin declensions he has to learn), *The He-Goat*, and *You Drunken Sot*. The quiet deadly satire of *The Classicist* (a skit on the reactionary critic Famintsyn) is a gem of its kind. *The Peep-show*, a long and elaborate lampoon on the foes of the national group, is entertaining, but cannot be understood without circumstantial explanations of the topical allusions (to Zaremba, the head of the Petersburg Conservatoire, to Famintsyn, to Serof, and others) with which it teems. Among the romantic-dramatic songs, pride of place goes to *The Songs and Dances of Death*:[1] above all *Trepak* (Death getting hold, on a stormy winter night, of a peasant, and whirling him into a wild dance; as his life ebbs, he dreams of a lovely summer day) and *Lullaby* (a dialogue between Death and a mother watching over her sick child). The other two, *Serenade* (Death the lover, wooing a maiden) and *The Commander in Chief* (Death's hymn of triumph as he surveys a corpse-strewn battle-field), do not quite rise to the same supremely high level, but are fine achievements none the less. So is *Forgotten*, inspired by a painting by Vereshchaghin, another telling evocation of a deserted battlefield. *On the Dnieper*, a war song of the Ukraine, also belongs to Mussorgsky's best.

[1] Certain Russian singers, by their interpretations of these songs (one of them revels in uncalled-for *parlandos*, " gags ", snorts, and grunts), have set a deplorable example. The first condition of adequate interpretation is thorough respect for Mussorgsky's texts and indications.

CHAPTER VIII

MUSSORGSKY (*continued*)

MUSSORGSKY completed only one work for the stage, *Boris Godunof*, his masterpiece. As early as 1858 he had started on an *Œdipus*, in which he soon lost interest; and in 1863 on a *Salammbo*, many portions of which he composed before deciding to give it up (some of the music was incorporated in later works). In 1868 he began to set to music Gogol's comedy *The Marriage* (it ought to be named, really, *Getting Married*), completing the first Act, in vocal score form, speedily, but soon afterwards deciding not to proceed any further, his plans for *Boris Godunof* having driven everything else out of his mind. *Boris* finished, he began *Khovanshchina*, and a little later a comic opera, *The Sorotchintsy Fair*, working fitfully now at the one, now at the other, until the end of his life.

He was delighted with his setting of *The Marriage*. To Rimsky-Korsakof he wrote:

> If you forget all operatic traditions and admit the principle of musical discourse carried out in all simplicity, *The Marriage* is an opera. If I have managed to render the straightforward expression of thoughts and feelings as it occurs in ordinary speech, and my rendering is musicianly and artistic, then the deed is done.

And a few years later to Stassof, presenting him with the manuscript of the work:

> Accept my *Marriage*, examine it, compare it with *Boris*, and you will see that what I give you is, irrevocably, my own self. I am convinced that to connoisseurs, it will reveal much as to my musical audacities.

He was thoroughly right. This little Act, consisting entirely of dialogue, stands unique in the repertory of music for the verve, piquancy, and humour of the characterization, the subtlety of the intonations, and the wealth of vivid pantomimic suggestions in the simple, straightforward accompaniment. As set down by Mussorgsky, for four singers and a piano, it is eminently suitable for performance in intimate surroundings. Attempts to orchestrate it have been made, with indifferent success; and also to supply the missing Acts. Of the latter only one, by Ippolitof-Ivanof, has been published. It is a dull, and rather laboured, affair.

Coming to *Boris Godunof*, we are faced with a situation unique in the history of opera. Mussorgsky first composed it at white heat, within little more than a twelve-month, without showing, it would seem, any portion of it to his friends and without receiving any advice from them. It was rejected by the Committee of the Imperial Theatres, being found objectionable from the artistic point of view and also for reasons of expediency. In 1871–1872, encouraged by suggestions from his friends, he remodelled it extensively, suppressing portions to which the State censorship might object, adding episodes and scenes that gave the singers more opportunities, and bringing the score closer to the approved type of grand opera.

By an amazing stroke of good fortune, the manuscripts of the suppressed or altered portions of the initial version were preserved: so that eventually Professor Lamm was able to reconstitute this version in full except for one brief, unimportant transition at the opening of Scene V.[1] This means we have two versions, between which there are many points of contact, but also differences great enough to make of them two distinct wholes, each of which should be appreciated on its own merits, without reference to the other. A comparison between them is bound to end in a deadlock. Each has beauties of its own, is superior to the other in certain respects and inferior in certain others. Both are self-sufficient and complete. The initial version is more close-knit from both the dramatic and the musical point of view. There is greater variety in the second. The first, shorter, less operatic, far more compact, consists almost entirely of dialogues and chorus. It shows us a much stronger Boris, much less addicted to self-pity; and its grimness and tension are absolutely unrelieved from start to finish, except for the full-flavoured comedy of the scene at the inn.

It consists of seven scenes only. In Scene I the people assembled in a square ask Boris to accept the throne. Scene II is that of his coronation. The third is in a monastery. An old monk, Pimen, and a novice, Grigory, are talking about the crime by which Boris secured the throne, and Grigory decides to impersonate the murdered Tsarevitch. Then comes a scene at an inn, during which we see Grigory, disguised, escaping into Lithuania, where he is going to begin plotting against Boris. Scene V shows Boris with his children, his conversation with Prince Shuisky (his chief counsellor and a

[1] See M. Mussorgsky: *Boris Godunof*. The complete original text edited, in accordance with the autograph manuscripts . . . by Paul Lamm. 1928, Russian State Edition; Oxford University Press. This is the only complete and reliable edition. It gives both the initial and the final versions in full.

relentless plotter against him), his remorse and the ghost of his victim haunting him.   Grigory is never seen again on the stage after his escape from the inn.   After he has become Dimitri, the Pretender, we just feel, in the background, his ominous presence.   Scene VI shows Boris in contact again with his people as on the day of his coronation; but this time, instead of hailing him, they tell him they suffer and beg him to give them bread; and, as they have heard of Dimitri's progress through Russia, they are ready to revolt against Boris.   Then comes a scene in the Council, a debate on measures to be taken against the Pretender, and the death of Boris in an agony of remorse and terror.

In the second version, the last section of Scene I (a very effective one) is cut out.   So is, in Scene III, the narrative, by Pimen, of the murder carried out by order of Boris—the very apex of the scene and one of the keystones of the whole opera.   Scene V is different, many of the additions constituting improvements; but the part of Tsar Boris has become decidedly less pithy and telling.   Scene VI is lacking.   In its stead, we have a whole act showing Dimitri the Pretender in Poland, plotting against Boris and courting Princess Marina.   The Council and death scene follows, and the opera ends with a magnificent evocation of the people in revolt and the Pretender marching against Moscow.

Despite the remodelling, the masterpiece did not find great favour with the public.   The opera-goers who sneered at it, and the critics who ran it down, would have laughed loud had they been told that a day would come when *Boris* would be regarded as the finest of all Russian operas, and Mussorgsky as the greatest of Russian composers.

For *Khovanshchina*, Mussorgsky outlined in 1873 an ambitious, complex plan.   He started work enthusiastically; but, whereas he had made a splendid, thoroughly workmanlike job of the libretto of *Boris* on the basis of Pushkin's play of the same title, here he failed in his attempt to cram into one opera a miscellany of materials, adequate treatment of which would have required a whole cycle of full-length operas.   At that time ill-health, the outcome of the drink habit he had acquired, while still in his teens, under the influence of disastrous surroundings (at a school for cadets, and afterwards during his brief military career), had impaired his capacity for sustained work.   And, naturally, the attempt to carry on simultaneously with *The Sorotchintsy Fair* had a disastrous effect on both undertakings.   He found himself compelled to shorten or leave out much of what he had composed or planned, thereby increasing the gaps and obscurities in the action.   Eventually, he managed to knock the first four Acts into shape; but of the fifth only a few fragments were put on paper. Rimsky-Korsakof revised, abridged, finished, and scored the work shortly after Mussorgsky's death, thereby rendering production possible; but many interesting points and beautiful things were swept away or spoilt in the process. In 1931, Lamm and Assafief published the genuine full text of the manuscript. There can be no question that in this unrevised form, the work, even if Mussorgsky had finished and scored it, would never have stood the test of performance. As a play, it is long-drawn; much of it consists of unconnected scenes. The music varies in quality. Some of it is feeble, but the greater part of it is as telling and beautiful from the musical point of view (that is, apart from its value for dramatic purposes or characterization) as anything in *Boris*.

It is carried out on broader and somewhat smoother lines, with fewer bold innovations and striking technical details. At times it is thinner in texture; and as a rule its pace is slower, in keeping with that of the action. Its dramatic significance is different from that of the *Boris* music, because its function is not the same. In *Boris* there is always action. The principal characters are ever doing something or tending somewhere. They are in motion, and the music co-operates. Here, practically nothing happens on the stage. Most scenes are illustrative rather than active—chapters from or illustrations to a chronicle rather than constituent parts of a drama. In other words, they are essentially characterization—characterization in which the music plays a big part, and which is achieved, not, as in *Boris*, by the subtle use of theme-transformations and derivations (an analysis of the functions of the three leitmotifs referring to Tsar Boris would require a whole chapter), but by means of no less subtly and effectively selected melodic designs and rhythms.

So, all told, the musical beauties of *Khovanshchina* are great and many. We must be willing to treasure them for their own sake, rather than as component parts of a dramatic score. Numerous are the scenes which, adequately and reverently scored, might grace the repertory of our concerts and broadcasts.

Of *The Sorotchintsy Fair*, Mussorgsky composed but disconnected fragments, some of them very attractive, others rather thin and commonplace. Among the best scenes in it are: a Market Scene, the music of which was first composed for an opera, *Mlada*, commissioned by the Director of the Imperial Theatres from four composers (the other three were Borodin, Cui, and Rimsky-Korsakof), each to contribute one act; and a splendid choral version of the tone-poem *A Night on the Bare Mountain*, introduced as an intermezzo evoking the dream-vision of one of the characters. And most people will agree with G. Abraham's view that "if *The Fair* was the work of a lesser man, we should welcome its sheaf of pleasant tunes, its grotesque humour and its charming colours without grumbling that it is no more than it is". After Mussorgsky's death, three composers in turn—Cui, N. Tcherepnin, and Shebalin—tried their hand at finishing the work, of which not even a full libretto existed. Tcherepnin's version is ably done from the musical point of view, but does not hold the stage. Shebalin's (Russian State Edition) is more substantial and better co-ordinated.

A long chapter would be required to deal with the posthumous fate of Mussorgsky's works; but only a bare outline of the strange and scandalous story can be given here. After his death, his music remained neglected for a long period, even *Boris Godunof* sinking into oblivion. Rimsky-Korsakof, who undertook to prepare for publication all the works of his that remained in manuscript, found that "they teemed with absurd, incoherent harmonies and part-writing, ill-chosen instrumentation, and other evidence of technical impotence; but they showed so much talent, originality, and vitality that it was imperative to publish them. Publication without a skilful hand to put them in order, however, would have had no sense except a biographico-historical one. What was needed was an edition for practical purposes, for making his colossal talent known, not merely his personality and sins against art." So he proceeded to remodel and correct, hardly a voice in Russia (nothing was known of Mussorgsky in any other country) being raised in protest. He also revised a good many of the works already published. In 1896 *Boris Godunof*, in a shockingly mutilated and appallingly bowdlerized form given to it by him, was produced in Petersburg. That same year, a gifted Russian singer, Maria Olenin, and her husband, Pierre d'Alheim, an author and lecturer, gave in Paris a set of lecture-recitals which introduced Mussorgsky's songs and excerpts from his operas to the musical public.

This propaganda they continued year after year, not only in France but in other countries, gaining for Mussorgsky a small but active and determined minority of champions. The movement spread so rapidly that when, in 1908, the Russian impresario Serge Diaghilef produced at the Paris Opera *Boris Godunof* (it was its first performance outside Russia) in Rimsky-Korsakof's mutilated and bowdlerized arrangement—further rearranged for the occasion —a storm of protests arose, Press and musical public clamouring for the genuine text. And, while a number of professionals, critics, composers, and theorists continued to harp upon Mussorgsky's alleged clumsiness and inefficiency, the ranks of his supporters were swelled by qualified judges whom nobody could suspect of inclining to suffer bungling gladly—Debussy, Ravel, Vincent d'Indy, and Tovey among others. In England events followed the same course. In 1905, as mentioned at the beginning of Chapter II (p. 17), the *Oxford History of Music* dismissed Mussorgsky with a couple of opprobrious epithets: in 1928 the critic of *The Times* devoted three-quarters of a column to explaining how Rimsky-Korsakof's correction of one of his " barbarous eccentricities " ruined the effectiveness of the passage in which it occurred. Equally significant is the fact that when *Boris Godunof* was still new to London (1912), Ernest Newman declared that " Mussorgsky was never more than half a musician in the sense in which we apply the word to composers like Wagner and Strauss, or even Gluck and Weber ". Twenty years later he proclaimed that " in the generation of about 1860–1890 the only unquestionably great composers of which Europe could boast were Wagner, Brahms, Berlioz, Mussorgsky and Verdi ".

Circumstances that had nothing to do with art, or even with scholastic art theories, delayed the recognition of the genuine *Boris*. Still, time continues to work in Mussorgsky's favour. And one may confidently expect that when normal circumstances again prevail, none of the works of his of which we have the full genuine text will ever be given in any spurious form.

It has been said that however great the demerits of the Rimsky-Korsakof revisions may be, they helped to make Mussorgsky's music known and appreciated at a time when the originals would have disconcerted the public. The opposite opinion—*viz.* that no better proof of the vitality of Mussorgsky's music could be found than the fact that it remained significant even after being disfigured; and that but for the revisions, the genuine texts would have been known and appreciated far sooner—has also found support. The truth seems to be that the revisions did serve a purpose in Russia, for whose musicians and musical public the originals were too strong meat. But in France there existed at least an experienced, progressively-minded minority, familiar enough with modern developments to be able to accept Mussorgsky on his own terms. They started vindicating his genius at a time when the garbled texts, already in possession of the field, stood very much in the way. The vindication would have been easier and speedier had the field been clear.

CHAPTER IX

RIMSKY-KORSAKOF

REALIZING the unquestionable fact that the national Russian style was created, in all its essentials, by Glinka and Balakiref, to be extended far beyond the scope of Rimsky-Korsakof's vision by Borodin and, especially, Mussorgsky, we still have to admit that Rimsky-Korsakof's music has a physiognomy distinctly its own. It is most attractive and interesting in many ways, disappointing in as many others. It reflects, not a single-minded and consistent artistic personality such as Balakiref's, Borodin's, or Mussorgsky's, but a complex, disconcerting mixture of contrasting, and indeed conflicting, elements. When studying the music of those three, one hardly ever feels one need turn to their biography: with Rimsky-Korsakof's, ever and anon the need for a biographical explanation makes itself felt. So much so that, at times, critics who did not know the true facts were lured into providing inaccurate reasons: for instance, when his third symphony was first given in Paris, one influential and conscientious critic averred that the work dated from a time when the composer had not yet found himself—the truth being that it dated from a time (1873) when, having already composed a number of highly characteristic works, he stood in danger of losing his personality for good and all through running counter to his real nature and striving to emulate the technical methods of the West at their most scholastic.

His attitude to his art, too, was different from theirs. As a boy, he says in his autobiography, he had a gift for music, but no special fondness for it. Then, he became passionately fond of it, and enjoyed " playing with it ". The expression is significant. To the end of his life music remained to him a fascinating, complex playing-field whose possibilities he eagerly explored, " playing with sounds, taking an almost childish delight in inventing combinations of chords and timbres, amusing himself by trying his strength in new directions " (Abraham, *Studies in Russian Music*). This does not mean that he lacked earnestness. On the contrary, a time was soon to come when he developed an inclination to over-earnestness. But it does mean that, all told, music was to him all make-believe; and that therefore, he did not always succeed in making it convincing to others.

At seventeen he was introduced to Balakiref, under whose guidance he started on his career enthusiastically. Soon he became a full-fledged member of the group. The orchestral works he composed during the next few years created a most favourable impression. Some of them, notably the tone-poem *Sadko* (1867), and the symphonic suite *Antar* (1868), belong, together with the later *Fairy Tale* (1880) and *Sheherazade* (1888), to the very best of his output. His first opera, *The Maid of Pskof*, was successfully produced in 1873. Yet, gradually, disenchantment crept in. He began to feel annoyed with himself for knowing far too little about his craft, and with Balakiref for not having helped him to acquire more knowledge, theoretical and practical.

> "Balakiref's attitude to his pupils was, I feel, altogether wrong. A gifted student requires but little help. It is easy to teach him all he needs. He should have given me a few lessons in harmony and counterpoint, made me write a few fugues, explained to me the syntax of musical form. But he could not do this, never having studied methodically, and holding that methodical study was not needful."—(*Autobiography*, with reference to 1862.)
> "I knew nothing. I could not harmonize a chorale properly, had never written a single counterpoint, did not know the names of all intervals and chords, and had but the haziest notion of the principles of form and of instrumental technique." (*Ib.*, with reference to 1871.)

And so, in proportion as the consciousness of his lack of crafts-manship developed within him, the desire grew to emulate Western composers on their own ground. He started to increase his technical efficiency by studying Tchaikovsky's newly-published handbook of harmony and the old-fashioned treatises of Cherubini and Beller-mann. Whether by following a course that corresponded to no reality within him, by studying the scholastic routine of working-out and building up and furbishing and polishing, he sacrificed some of his own inborn qualities, acquiring fluency and conventional correctness at the expense of the spontaneity and vigour he had asserted in his earlier work, is a moot question, all the more difficult to solve for the reason that the primitive versions of the works with which he first made his mark are not accessible. *Sadko* he revised in 1869 and again in 1892; *Antar* in 1875 and again in 1897; the first symphony in 1884; *The Maid of Pskof* in 1875–76, then in 1877, and further again in 1891. So we cannot compare the various versions as we can Mussorgsky's genuine *Boris Godunof* and Rimsky-Korsakof's revision of it, in order to determine the rights and wrongs of the alterations. It may be noted that *Antar*, performed in Paris and Brussels (1889 and 1890) in its first form, came off with flying colours—a significant fact.

Anyhow, the truth seems to be that nature had not intended him to progress along the lines he elected to follow. In respect of form-building and working-out, Borodin had found his own solution, a highly satisfactory and original one, not one provided in any technical handbook; so had Balakiref. Mussorgsky's interests lay in another direction, but he too did find splendid solutions of his particular problems. Rimsky-Korsakof, instead of seeking, for better or for worse, within himself, decided in favour of the cut-and-dried solution supplied by treatises of composition. He had no capacity for assimilating the fundamental principles out of which the mechanics of routine craftsmanship had developed; more often than not his would-be working-out is mere spinning-out; repetition and dilution, not live growth. He never succeeded in adding much to his inborn assets, or in acquiring that architectural sense to which he aspired. His power lay in other directions. Ernest Newman, the French critic Gaston Carraud, and other competent judges hold that he excelled chiefly in the province of melodic invention. This view is true to a great extent, but Abraham's contention that many of his melodies are " synthetic rather than spontaneous, and deliberately borrowed or calculated " should not be overlooked. Nor is his harmony particularly original, or even telling. All in all, it is to its brilliant, many-hued, wonderfully diverse colour-schemes, to his skill in manipulating and contrasting the elements he uses, and above all to a certain verve, that his music owes much of its character and fascination. He had a rare capacity for indulging in unconstrained, ingenious, infectious musical fun.

Maybe it is in his early works that he is at his best: especially the orchestral ones. There is nothing, in Russian music or in that of any other country, quite like *Sadko*, with its riotous pageantry of dances; *Antar*, with the diversity of vivid imagery in its first three movements and the moving, wistful poetry of its finale, built on a lovely Arabian tune; or *Fairy Tale* (1880), with its wealth of picturesque, ever-shifting fancies and dream-visions; to which must be added the *Spanish Capriccio* (1887), the *Easter Overture*, and *Sheherazade* (both 1888), the last three instrumental works he was to compose: the first a coruscation of the brightest orchestral colours, the second partly mystical, but mostly an evocation of the pagan rejoicings that mark the Easter Day celebration in Russia, the autobiography explains; and the third—the best known of all his works—a succession of delightfully racy tone-pictures, culminating in a most exciting finale.

They do not go very deep, no doubt: the finale of *Antar* remains something unique in his output. But of their kind they are supreme and perfect. They show him thoroughly at ease, carefree, always to the point. Not a sign of the deficiencies noticeable elsewhere mars our enjoyment of them.

Several other orchestral works of his, less exciting, provide opportunities for more tranquil enjoyment; for instance, the *Sinfonietta* on Russian folk-tunes (1885), and especially the terse, more substantial, and more closely knit Piano Concerto (1882).

A survey of the series of his operas (fourteen in number, including the one-act *Vera Sheloga*, composed in 1898 as a prologue to *The Maid of Pskof*), leaves one with mixed impressions. After 1888, opera became his principal sphere of activity, the other works of the period (chiefly vocal music) being of secondary inportance. Were it not for the high level he reached in parts of *Mlada* (1890) and *Sadko* (1896), based on the same legend as his tone-poem of 1868, in *Kitej* (1904), and in *The Golden Cockerel* (1907), one would be justified in saying that nothing he turned out after 1888 can compare with his previous achievements. There is some attractive music in most of the operas, but the pace is often slow, the substance thin; there is a good deal of dilution, of spinning-out of ideas not always very significant in themselves. He held that " opera was first and foremost a musical composition ", and had no real feeling for the requirements of dramatic music. Even in the music of the delightful *Snow-Maiden*, Gerald Abraham rightly points out, there is " no trace of [symbolic] meaning, and little of definite emotion ". And Ernest Newman, referring to certain arias that reveal his gift for melodic invention at its best, is forced to confess that " the enchantment of those things does not depend on which character sings them, or at which stage of the dramatic action they occur, or to what words they are written or what phase of psychology they illustrate: their enchantment depends solely on themselves ".

His autobiography and his letters show that he was not unaware of these deficiencies. In 1891 he decided that the music of *Mlada* was " as cold as ice ". He saw in many of his works " not real live music, but cold, deliberate fabrication ". At the very time when he was about to start work on *The Golden Cockerel*, he wondered whether it was not high time for him to give up composition altogether. Yet he felt convinced that he had found the right path away from his early faith: " it was only because of my study of technique that new, life-giving currents flowed into my music, and that I was able to make headway ", the autobiography says.

The following comparison between the Balakiref circle and the circle of composers grouped around the publisher Belaief in the 'eighties and after is most characteristic:

> Balakiref's circle was revolutionary, Belaief's progressive. It consisted of composers feeble in technique, amateurs almost: Belaief's, on the contrary, of well-trained musicians. Balakiref's was intolerant and exclusive, Belaief's liberal and eclectic. Its members set great store by technical perfection; but they too opened new roads, building them less hastily, more securely.

It would have been better for him to resist the lure of eclecticism. His weakest works are the most eclectic in style: the third symphony, the operas *Servilia*, *Pan Voyevoda* on non-Russian subjects, and *The Tsar's Bride*, in which he adheres to all the conventions of Western grand opera.

The weakest parts of *Mlada*, *Sadko*, and *Kitej* are those that show his temporary allegiance to Wagner. In other words, his eclectic music is a kind of half-way house; and this may help to explain why it is so difficult to judge it fairly. With Balakiref, Borodin, and Mussorgsky, set standards are of no avail: we must either accept their music for what it is or not accept it at all. His, on the contrary, invites reference to certain set standards because he observes certain conventions of which, however, he seems to be the slave rather than the master—whence the impression of " cold, deliberate fabrication ". One cannot help feeling that he, who sought to renounce the methods of Russian nationalism " for the sake of freedom of style ", is never so free as when he keeps to those methods without ever an afterthought.

Again, in opera, his greatest asset, as a rule, is his love for " playing with music ": for instance, in the carnival and sun-worship scenes in *Snow-Maiden* (one cannot help feeling how deeply he must have enjoyed writing them) and the charmingly poetic bird-music and spring-music in the same opera; the comic and fantastic scenes that occur in nearly all the operas; the racy crowd scenes in *Mlada*, *Sadko*, and *Kitej*; the pagan ceremonies and phantasmagoria in *Mlada*, and the underseas pageantry and dances in *Sadko* (most of the music of these is built up out of the elements of his tone-poem of 1868). In *Kitej* there are many fine things, including nature-music which he must have composed in the same mood of deep spiritual enjoyment as the nature-music in *Snow-Maiden*.

In *Tsar Saltan* (1900) and *The Golden Cockerel* (1907) there is plenty of musical fun of a restrained and polished kind; he aimed at atticism rather than at the display of animal spirits.

Psychological and dramatic characterization do not come within the scheme of most of these operas. The libretti keep to an atmosphere of pure fairy-tale—and indeed the purely picturesque atmosphere of Grimm rather than the more human and emotional tone of Hans Andersen—or of light comedy without under-currents. Leaving aside *The Tsar's Bride*, *Servilia*, and *Pan Voyevoda*, whose libretti are of the neither-fish-nor-flesh stereotyped order, we may say that only *The Maid of Pskof* and *Kitej* provided opportunities for the expression of dramatic emotion.

The Maid of Pskof is the most dramatic of all. The greater part of the music was composed at a time when Rimsky-Korsakof shared a flat with Mussorgsky, who was then engaged in composing the second version of *Boris Godunof*. And in many respects the music—especially in the choral scenes and in the treatment of Tsar Ivan the Terrible's part—has affinities with that of Mussorgsky's masterpiece. In *Kitej* the character of Fevronia, the simple, gentle maiden, her mystic faith in life and in the world that God made, the world " in which He is everywhere ", is most convincingly evoked in simple, loftily poetic music. And in his treatment of the part of Grishka Kuterma, the drunkard, ever obsessed by dread visions and nameless terrors, he has found accents and colours as telling, and as grimly realistic, as anything in *The Maid of Pskof*. The final mystic scene in the city of Kitej is one of the finest things he ever wrote.

CHAPTER X

TCHAIKOVSKY, ARENSKY, RACHMANINOF

HARDLY anybody has discussed Tchaikovsky without exaggerating either his qualities or his defects. There was a time, not so far back, when he was regarded, in Western countries, as the only Russian composer worth noticing, the only one who had tackled music competently and in an earnest, respectable spirit; who was not a " barbarian " and a " musical cannibal ", but wrote music that could easily be understood and enjoyed. He was popular in Germany at a time when Balakiref, Mussorgsky, Borodin, and Rimsky-Korsakof were unknown or despised, and in England when these other composers were still regarded, at best, as interesting examples of exotic singularity and waywardness. The general attitude towards him at the end of the nineteenth century will be shown by the following two excerpts.

He has profitably studied, with keen, unspoilt receptivity, the masterpieces of the West, especially those of melodious Italy and, above all, of more thoughtful Germany. He does not profess to belong to the new Russian school, but he is thoroughly and unmistakably Russian. He commands both a glowing imagination and a technical mastery that enables him to be quite at home in every province of his art. In every one of his compositions one feels the presence of the divine spark.

(Otto Neitzel, in 1890.)

His creative genius displays itself under the three headings of orchestral, dramatic, and lyrical music, in all of which he achieved high excellence. His productiveness, too, was immense: nothing like it—in such universal perfection as his— can be instanced since Mozart. He had an exquisite perception for finish and detail. In his capacity for patient labour, he was singularly unlike the generality of his compatriots. He stands wide apart from Glinka or any of the exponents of the Russian school proper . . . who often are little short of hideous in their daring efforts.

(A. E. Keeton, in the *Contemporary Review*, July 1900.)

Meanwhile, in France, the only country in which, at the time, the music of the " Russian school proper " was known to, and greatly appreciated by, at least a minority of keen music-lovers, a widely different view prevailed, and Tchaikovsky's music was unfavourably contrasted with theirs by those who missed in it the very qualities that rendered the masterpieces of the nationalist Russians so significant and attractive. This view, maybe, was neither reasonable nor fair. Most of the Russian nationalists held Tchaikovsky's music in high esteem, and did not feel that the differences between it and theirs precluded admiration for its merits.

Still, there can be no denying that the differences are many and serious. Referring to Hubert Parry's dictum that " Russian music naturally appealed to the awakening intelligence of the musical masses by vehement emotional spontaneity, orgiastic frenzy, dazzling effects of colour, barbaric rhythms, and unrestrained abandonment to physical excitement ", Gerald Abraham (in *Studies in Russian Music*) shrewdly points out that " the one man who had no sounder elements in his make-up, and of whom Parry was chiefly thinking, was Tchaikovsky ".

Eventually, the tide began to turn in other countries too. In the *Oxford History of Music* (Vol. VI, 1905) Tchaikovsky was described as " weak in the matters of concentration and sense of balance and design ". In 1906, Hadow wrote:

> Among the principal Russian masters, Tchaikovsky is, perhaps, the least central and the least representative; the want of personal force which enfeebled his life renders his music liable to external influences, and allows it sometimes, from very weariness of invention, to sink into triviality and commonplace. But, although the most unequal among great composers, he reaches, at his best, an extraordinarily high level of beauty.

And, while the popularity of Tchaikovsky's music with the listening public at large went on steadily increasing, so did— although on a small scale, and chiefly in professional circles—the number of those who regarded a good deal of this music as loose, cheap, over-emotional and sensational; who were more sensitive to its defects than to its merits, and so, maybe, failed no less grossly to hold the balance even than had the uncritical admirers of the earlier period.

Their attitude can be explained by borrowing an ingenious and forcible simile from Ernest Newman's *The Man Liszt*: " Every composer's mind has a certain odour, so to speak, that either strikes pleasantly on our nostrils or does not: it is the somewhat corrupt odour of Meyerbeer's mind, for instance, that makes some of us turn away from him today ". So did the "odour" of Tchaikovsky's mind turn a few of us away from him. It is a moot question whether any useful arguments could be adduced in support of this feeling—for it is, when all is said and done, a matter of feeling. The important point is that quite a number have been adduced, and that now the challengers are challenged in turn on their own ground: on questions not of feeling, but of musical facts.

The first to protest was Stravinsky, who in various writings, and especially in his *Memoirs*, enthusiastically praised, not only Tchaikovsky's genius generally, but his sense of form and design, and his dignity and restraint—that is, the very qualities that many were denying him. In the *Memoirs* Stravinsky writes:

> Tchaikovsky, while using Russian vernacular tunes, did not scruple to Frenchify them or Italianize them, as Glinka had done. The nationalists, on the contrary, followed in the wake of Wagner, Liszt, and Berlioz. In *Mavra*, I went straight back to Glinka—Tchaikovsky, following their example, reverting to the sound tradition established by them, and asserting my opposition to the nationalist creed.

But even before the publication of the *Memoirs*, many signs had shown that the tide had turned again. Thus, in 1924, Sir Hamilton Harty had written:

> Tchaikovsky's huge and sudden popularity in this country could hardly have endured at its height unless he had been the greatest composer who had ever lived. Such a fierce concentration of limelight on any one composer would have showed up the flaws in a far greater figure. The subsequent subsidence in the "Tchaikovsky craze" was a natural consequence of a somewhat exaggerated appreciation. But with all his faults, Tchaikovsky is again finding a settled and important place in our musical life. It would be absurd to claim for him the title of great composer, but he is the best of his kind, and the best of anything has always a settled value.

Of late, many critics (chiefly Russian) incline, with Stravinsky, to see only his merits. and to regard strictures on his form, style, and methods generally as unfounded. Thus D. Zhitomirsky, in *Sovietskaya Muzyka* :

> He was the first Russian symphonist of his kind, the first to write symphonies whose form was determined not by picturesque

imagery or impressions, not by ornamental colour-schemes or descriptive purposes, but by philosophical problems conceived in the abstract—one whose music has a tremendous force as well as a great historical value.

But it is in the pages of Tovey's *Essays in Musical Analysis* devoted to the Pathetic Symphony that we find the most strongly and most judicially substantiated vindication of Tchaikovsky on purely/ musical grounds, in flat contradiction of all that had ever been said about this particular work's looseness of form and meretriciousness of style:

> Nowhere else has he concentrated so great a variety of music within so effective a scheme; and the slow finale, with its complete simplicity of despair, is a stroke of genius which solves all the artistic problems that have proved most baffling to symphonic writers since Beethoven. The whole work carries conviction without the slightest sense of.effort; and its most celebrated features . . . are thrown into high relief by developments far more powerful, terse, and highly organized than Tchaikovsky has achieved in any other work.

It is rather disappointing to find Tovey explaining in a further essay, that the problems he referred to were merely " the problems of getting up any sense of movement in a finale at all ". Still, there can be no doubt that the distinguished analyst (whom nobody would regard as uncritical), while readily acknowledging that " Tchaikovsky was primarily a writer of light music, and that his tragedy was melodrama ", is not in the least put off by defects with which a number of listeners and critics have no patience.

It is quite true that Tchaïkovsky was primarily a writer of light music. He was nurtured as much on Gounod, Bizet, Delibes, and Massenet as on Glinka: and it is to those French influences as much as to his own nature that his naïve faith in the power of the obvious—even the most hackneyed kind of obvious—is to be traced back. Ballet-music of the then usual type had a special attraction for him. Its patterns and lilts are ever cropping up in his own music, in and out of place. And one cannot help feeling that while composing, he kept thinking of the effect his music would have upon audiences. Consequently, he was too easily satisfied with any musical idea that struck him as impressive or pleasing, however trite and cheap it might be.

And this, perhaps, is even more palpable in his most earnest, most self-confessional outpourings: listeners whom these leave unconvinced will, as often as not, find them intolerably bombastic, although there can be no questioning the 'sincerity of his purpose in them. Or maybe they will incline, with Gerald Abraham, to make allowances for the fact that " the impression of somewhat-less-than greatness we get from Tchaikovsky's biggest and most tragic works may be due to his not having had at his command a musical speech adequate to express what he wanted to say; but it is also caused by his morbid egotism, his inability to be universal ".

The list of his works is a long one, and comprises examples of nearly every order of music. Those who know, if not the whole, at least the greater part of that enormous output will probably agree with Hadow that at his best he reaches an extraordinary level of beauty,. although it may not be the kind of beauty to which they happen to be most sensitive.

The works most likely to enjoy lasting favour are the instrumental ones, and chiefly the orchestral. First and foremost the symphonies, especially the second, fourth and sixth (the " Pathetic "); the three piano concertos (two of them at present overshadowed by the ever-popular first, in B flat minor) and the violin concerto; the programmatic and other dramatic works—*Romeo and Juliet, Francesca da Rimini, Manfred, Hamlet*; and above all the ballets *The Swan Lake, The Sleeping Beauty* and *Casse-Noisette*. The chamber-music is little known nowadays. Findeisen, in Cobbett's *Cyclopedic Survey*, has high praise for the three string quartets and the piano trio in memory of N. Rubinstein. The piano music and the songs (over a hundred in number) are of secondary importance. The choral music, which includes a Liturgy of St. John Chrysostom and other church-music, has long remained overlooked. Of the nine operas, two, *Eugen Onieghin* and *The Queen of Spades*, have a value as period-pieces. In the first-named, Tchaikovsky's gift of melodic invention (limited in scope, but genuine so far as it goes) is displayed at its best.

Abraham has ably solved the delicate problem of holding the balance even in his summing-up of the Tchaikovsky case:—

> Tchaikovsky's current of thought seems rather anæmic at times, but it always flows naturally. The unique fascination the *Pathétique* exercises on the semi-musical is largely due to the intensity of its life: there is not a bar in it that is not musically alive. He owed his original popularity in Russia to the admiration of the numerous people of ordinary intelligence and not fastidious taste . . . to the same class, equally inno-cent of artistic snobbery and artistic discernment, who still

think very highly of him in England. He had . . . a great melodic gift and a wonderful flair for orchestration (apart from his outbursts of sheer brutal noise) ; a mediocre harmonic sense [N.B.: his shortcomings in this respect make themselves acutely felt whenever he deals with folk-tunes], little power of development or genuine architecture, but a marvellous power for filling a big canvas with living music. In opera as in the symphony, he had a fatal weakness: inability to escape from himself and his own feelings. He will always be ranked higher by those who find an artist more interesting than his art than by those who care immensely for art, and very much less for artistic personalities.

Rosa Newmarch (who in the 'nineties and after did a good deal to make Tchaikovsky's music known in this country) comes to a similar conclusion in her article in Grove's *Dictionary* :—

His music, with its strange combination of the sublime and the platitudinous, will always touch the average hearer, to whom music is more a matter of feeling than of thought.

Likewise, from a slightly different angle, Ernest Newman :

He will always remain an interesting and sympathetic subject for the student. With all their faults, *Onieghin*, *The Queen of Spades*, and *Mazeppa* will always find a soft spot in the heart of a few people who can look beyond the actual achievement to the processes of the mind that lies at the back of these works.

Tchaikovsky's influence made itself felt far and wide: chiefly on the lesser Russians, beginning with Arensky and Rachmaninof, on Glazunof in the later part of his career, and to a degree on Gretchaninof: but also outside Russia, notably on Sibelius, of all people in the world. It is true that now and then the Finnish master, in his uninspired moods, often tends to imitation; his biographer, Cecil Gray, has noted that he occasionally followed in the footsteps not only of Tchaikovsky, but of Wagner, Grieg, Brahms, and even Strauss. Needless to say it is the defects rather than the qualities of the model that loom large in the imitations: with Sibelius, for instance, the coarse scoring of certain loud climaxes (first movement of first symphony, finale of second, etc.) with blaring brass and banging drums very much *à la* Tchaikovsky.

Anton Arensky (1861–1906) underwent, besides Tchaikovsky's influence, that of Rimsky-Korsakof, his teacher, as shown by the way in which he uses Russian and Eastern folk-tunes in his operas *A Dream of the Volga* and *Nala and Damayanti,* and his ballet *Egyptian Night.* His output includes two symphonies, the cantata *The Fountain at Bakhchisarai,* a good deal of piano music, and chamber-music. His first piano trio enjoyed a measure of popularity. The second movement of his string quartet in A minor, a set of variations on a Tchaikovsky theme, is by far the finest (one might well say, the one and only really fine) thing he ever wrote.

Serghei Rachmaninof (1873–1943) stands in the direct line of succession to Tchaikovsky, being no less self-centred, subjective, and romantic in disposition; and, as to style, eclectic and cosmopolitan. Although vernacular elements appear in his music and he did not fight shy of the innovations that were cropping up around him, he is, even more than Tchaikovsky, conservative and non-national; and therefore it might have been more appropriate to deal with him in Chapter XII, jointly with Medtner, Taneief, and others in whose music Western features overshadow any Slavonic element that may be present. Still, he stands so close to Tchaikovsky, and to Tchaikovsky alone among all the Russians, that maybe it is better to deal with him at this point. His mind is more disciplined, and his imagination less vivid. His fluency is unfailing, and never does anything in his music convey the sense of strain and effort that Tchaikovsky's now and then suggests.

His architectural sense is greater, but the materials he uses are less significant. One commentator, on praise intent, once wrote:

> Of the many abilities that go to the making of musical talent, he has one developed to a supreme pitch: imagination. And by imagination I mean an unusually rich supply of images and the power to marshal them. At an early age, he had an ear that needed no training and a memory that required no cultivation. So he acquired a rich store of sound-images before his formal training began.

Thus worded, the remark cuts both ways. It stresses the power to store and marshal images, but not the power to create them, which of course is the main thing. Stored images, after all, are but such stuff as rhetoric, rather than genuine eloquence, is made on. Opinion varies as to the part played by rhetoric and eloquence respectively in Rachmaninof's works—especially the later ones. After hearing the third symphony (1937), the critic R. Hull, a keen investigator of Rachmaninof's music, declared: "One realizes how much beauty can yet be spoken in the spacious terms of yesterday." Other critics felt otherwise; Capell, of the *Daily Telegraph*, among others:

> A palace without royalty. Rachmaninof still gives parties on the grand old scale, but no gorgeous guests turn up: the scene looks empty.

Apart from his piano music, which is in a class by itself, his most representative works are the second and third symphonies (the second is the most self-confessional of all his compositions), the *Variations on a Corelli Theme*, the second and third piano concertos, the cantatas *The Bells* (after Poe), and *Spring* and the tone-poems *The Rock* and *The Island of the Dead* (after a painting by Boecklin). His only two published ventures into the province of chamber-music, an Elegiac Trio in memory of Tchaikovsky (1893) and a 'cello sonata, also belong to the best of his output. The piano music does not, like Balakiref's, Debussy's, or Ravel's, break new ground either from the æsthetic or the technical point of view. It keeps within the Chopin–Schumann tradition; but within those boundaries what the composer sets out to do he does well. The *Morceaux de Fantaisie* op. 3 (containing the famous prelude in C sharp minor), the sets of Preludes op. 23 and 32 and of *Études-Tableaux* op. 33 and 39 will certainly continue to hold their own in the current repertory.

CHAPTER XI

LIADOF, GLAZUNOF, AND THE LESSER NATIONALISTS

MOST of the characteristic features of the vernacular Russian style are present in the music of Anatol Liadof (1855–1914) and the early works of Alexander Glazunof (1865–1936). Liadof was as Russian as any of his elders, and so he remained to the end of his life. Although he achieved comparatively little, he stands high among composers of his generation. Nature had bestowed upon him every conceivable gift except energy and perseverance. He had genuine poetic imagination and an unerring sense of music. Works such as his tone-picture *From the Book of Revelation* and his *Nénie* (Dirge) for orchestra show that he was capable of lofty, sustained eloquence, and could have done much more and shown greater versatility had he been more industrious and ambitious.

His other orchestral works are neither on a big scale nor far-reaching in scope. Ingenuity, alertness, poetic fancy, charm, and polish, are their chief merits. His tone-poems *Baba-Yaga* (" the witch "), *Kikimora* (the name of a goblin), and *The Enchanted Lake*, and his orchestral arrangements of Russian folk-tunes fully deserve a place in the sun; nor should his early *Mazurka* (a tone-picture of countryside revels), his *Ballad*, and his *Polonaise in Memory of Pushkin* be forgotten by concert-givers.

His piano music consists chiefly of short pieces, many of them delightful, and eminently suitable for home performance or performance in intimate circles. A few of his songs—and especially the charming songs for children op. 14, 18, 22—could hold their own on the concert platform. His choral compositions are few, but most attractive.

Glazunof's course resembles Rimsky-Korsakof's in one respect: he started his career under the banner of nationalism, and his early works stand in close relation to those of his elders in the group; but later he worked away from it, and his output, from the moment he reached the age of thirty, suggests Western rather than Russian affinities.

Not consciously, it would seem: for, at a time when critics in Western Europe were deploring his change of front, and ascribing it to the influence of Brahms and Reger, he expressed (in a conversation with the present writer) his regret at seeing Russian music gradually losing its national character, and composers following in the wake of German academicism. What happened within him is practically impossible to determine. No memoirs, no correspondence, no writings of his are available to help us. He was certainly not affected, like Rimsky-Korsakof, by a sense of technical inferiority: on the contrary, he rose to a high level of craftsmanship with surprising ease and speed. At seventeen, he composed a symphony that was enthusiastically received (it was published only after several revisions). At twenty, he had to his credit two string quartets, and half a dozen other orchestral works, including two fine Overtures on Greek folk-tunes and a splendid tone-poem, *Stenka Razin*. Other works followed in quick succession. His reputation rose steadily, spread through Europe to the United States, endured a fairly long while, but afterwards decreased, until a time came when his music was relegated more or less to the background. It is nowadays far less known than it ought to be.

By the time he was forty the catalogue of his works included eight symphonies, half a dozen big chamber works, three ballets, and a quantity of other works—over eighty opus numbers.

He was essentially a composer of instrumental music. He never was attracted by opera, and the small amount of vocal music he turned out is of no particular account. Of the early works, the most interesting are the second, third, and fourth symphonies and the tone-poems. They do not break new ground, but they are imaginative and full-blooded music, worthy of being regarded as original and not derivative. Especially so the tone-poems, and other works of the picturesquely descriptive order, which for raciness and drive stand close to Rimsky-Korsakof's. *The Forest*, with its evocations of the fairies, goblins, dwarfs, and giants of Slavonic mythology, is a companion-piece to the latter's *Fairy-Tale*, but stands in its own right. There is a wealth of telling imagery and poetic suggestions in the exciting *Eastern Rhapsody* (1885). *Stenka Razin* (1885), one of the most close-knit tone-poems inspired by a circumstantial programme, is a consummate example of thoroughly traditional form, built almost entirely on the famous song of the Volga boatmen (first published by Balakiref in 1866), the first two periods of which are used as subjects of the introduction and the allegro that follows, the third being kept in reserve for the peroration, and a Persian tune being used from the middle section onwards. *The Kremlin* (1890) and *The Sea* (1889) are less interesting, and the suite *The Middle Ages* (1902) is on a conventional level throughout; but the tone-picture *Spring* (1891) has a charm quite its own. It is one of the works that show his rare capacity for landscape painting.

Others are the introduction in *Stenka Razin*, probably devised under the influence óf the superb opening of Balakiref's *Tamara*, but certainly no mere pasticcio; and the poetic eventide evoked at the beginning of the *Eastern Rhapsody*. In *The Forest* there are very effective suggestions of setting and atmosphere.

Stenka Razin is not the only one of his earliest works showing his interest in problems of form and theme-manipulation. The piano suite *S-A-S-C-H-A* (a pet name for Alexander, the letters of which, in German nomenclature, correspond—S being accepted as ES, as in Schumann's *Lettres Dansantes*—to the notes E flat-A-E flat-C-B-A) consists of a Prelude, a Scherzo, a Waltz, and a Nocturne, all built on the main theme derived from the title. Most of the materials used in the Second Symphony (1886) are transformations, carried out thoroughly *à la* Liszt, of the opening theme. The result is most attractive; and it is a great pity that this symphony should be so thoroughly neglected.

Theme-transformations play a big part in the Suite for string quartet (op. 35). In the fourth quartet (op. 64) he resorts, not to simple theme-transformations in the Lisztian manner, but to the " cyclic " methods of the Franck–d'Indy school, according to which most of the themes are derived from a germ-cell or germ-cells given in the exposition of the opening movement. Here, the germ-cells are two in number. Although the derived themes are not particularly distinctive, the music is substantial, and the interest sustained. Being gifted with a true sense of symphonic treatment and working-out, he never resorts, as Rimsky-Korsakof did, to mere spinning-out and dilution. What he achieves may be more or less interesting (whether it comes off or not seems to be a matter of chance), but it is the genuine article, and not a makeshift substitute. He is very systematic about it all; and at this new stage, his music is characterized by greater deliberation and slower pace.

That interest in form problems which plays so great a part in his make-up becomes now and then too abstract: the problems are not the outcome of idiosyncrasies of his materials, as was the case with Borodin (Second Symphony) and Balakiref (*Tamara*, *Islamey*, etc.). He seems to plan the task first and devise suitable materials afterwards : for instance, the main subjects of his quintet op. 39 and his eighth symphony are long phrases lending themselves to division into motifs to be treated separately (as in *Stenka Razin*, but the outcome is far less significant). On the contrary, the main theme of his second piano sonata consists merely of two descending fifths, B-E, G-C, an altogether neutral germ-cell, predetermining no special course of treatment.

These various experiments, and also his incursions into the folk-lore of various countries (his later output includes a *Finnish Fantasy, Finnish Sketches,* and a *Karelian Legend* for orchestra), betoken an enquiring mind. But his disposition was not really adventurous. Had it been, he would have been able, with his splendid technical equipment (which included a sense of polyphony such as few Russians, and certainly no Russian nationalist, commanded), to make great progress towards the discovery of new methods of modal polyphony.

But it was not to be: past a certain point, he inclined to follow the line of least resistance—as in his third symphony, when, having aroused expectations by presenting a modal theme in the slow introduction, he frankly goes back to the usual major as soon as the allegro starts.

In later life, he composed comparatively little. He showed here and there a tendency to introspection, to effusions not dissimilar to Tchaikovsky's, although more restrained and less self-confessional: in the fifth quartet, for instance, and also the *Song of Fate* for orchestra. In two orchestral Preludes in memory of Stassof (op. 85, no. 1) and Gogol (op. 87) he strikes a new imaginative note; the *Stassof* prelude especially is rich in recondite poetic suggestiveness. The Prelude in memory of Rimsky-Korsakof is rather Wagnerian in tone-character. The sixth symphony is a particularly fine example of technical efficiency, with the ingenious variations in its slow movement and the elaborate polyphony of the finale, in which an old Church chant is used.

Serghei Liapunof (1859–1924) was very much influenced by Balakiref. In fact, his idiom and technique are entirely derivative: still, he succeeded in displaying a poetic feeling and a sense of colour quite his own, especially in his songs and piano music. His nature was fundamentally lyrical and contemplative. Like Balakiref, he found inspiration in the atmosphere and scenery of the Caucasus and the folk-music of old Russia; but his composition on a big scale (two piano concertos, two symphonies, tone-poems, etc.) show that he was not gifted with an architectural vision enabling him to achieve formal unity. His saving grace lay in his sense of melody and harmony, of writing for the voice and for the instruments, and in his capacity for heroic eloquence and attractive colour-play. These gifts are manifest even in the big works, which, however, are unlikely to maintain a place in the repertory. His songs and piano music (and above all the superb set of *Études d'Exécution Transcendante*) and songs will certainly keep his memory alive.

Alexander Gretchaninof (b. 1864) is the first Russian composer of distinction who sprang from the ranks of the people. According to his autobiography, his father was a shopkeeper in a small way, who could read but not write; and his mother learnt to read only after having grown up.

His secular music, in many respects, stands close to Liadof's, having the same qualities of simple ingenuity, delicacy of touch, shapeliness, expressiveness, and restraint. On the other hand, a certain softness, a tendency to lapse into the facile and obvious, or to indulge in declamatory outbursts (as in the final section of his well-known song *The Steppe*) betray now and then the influence of Tchaikovsky (but never of his pessimism and gloom).

The catalogue of his works is a long one. It comprises four symphonies; a violin and a piano concerto; four string quartets and other chamber-music; two operas (*Dobrynia Nikititch*, on a Russian legendary subject, and *Sister Beatrice*, after Maeterlinck's play); a quantity of choral and other vocal music, and of piano music; and a good deal of church-music, notably three settings, for various combinations, of the Liturgy of St. John Chrysostom, and, for the Roman Catholic liturgy, a *Missa Œcumenica*, a *Missa Festiva*, a Mass for children's voices and organ, and a set of six motets. Music for children or about children, vocal and instrumental, constitutes a large part of his output; and that fraction of it which is generally known (only a very small one) has won wide appreciation. There is a growing feeling that, together with the sacred music, it constitutes the most valuable part of his production. The works intended for the Orthodox service are very fine, but not suitable for concert performance. Those intended for the Roman Church are not yet available for study. According to Joseph Yasser in the *Musical Quarterly* (July 1942), they contain much that is of high artistic value, and many interestingly original features—especially so, he says, the *Missa Œcumenica*.

Gretchaninof is, at the time of writing, settled in the United States: the works he has composed in that country have not yet reached us.

Vassili Kalinnikof (1866–1901) died long before having given his full measure. His principal works are two symphonies, a tone-picture, *The Cedar and the Palm-tree*, a few fine songs, a string quartet, a choral Cantata, *St. John Chrysostom*, a ballad, *The Russalka*, for solo, voice, chorus, and orchestra, and an opera, *1812*. Only the first symphony (in G minor) has achieved popularity. In this and other works, he shows affinities with Borodin. (Slonimsky, in *Music since 1900*, describes him as " a composer of melodious national music approaching in a diluted form the grandeur of Borodin ".) It is worth noting that he told the critic Kruglikof that he had sedulously studied Glinka's music, but was not acquainted with that of Borodin.

His temperament was essentially lyrical; and in his music the expression of subjective emotions plays a big part, although never a melodramatic one. On the other hand, he often found inspiration in the atmosphere, aspects, traditions, and folk-music of the cities and countryside of his native land, the old-world government of Orel, and of the Crimea, where he spent the last five years of his life. So he was as spontaneous and natural in his use of the vernacular as any of his elders. It is deplorable that his music should remain so generally neglected.

Another sad case is that of Vladimir Senilof (1875–1918). None of his major works were published, and most of them were never performed, despite the interest aroused in musical circles by the few that were. The manuscripts of three operas, several symphonic works (among them the tone-poems *Mtsyri, Pan, The Scythians*), three string quartets, and a number of other works, are preserved in the Leningrad Public Library. "Many of these", Andrei Rimsky-Korsakof says, "stand out not only for their technical merits but for the genuine talent displayed in them. A time will come when they will be found worthy of careful consideration." The critic Karatyghin, too, has high praise for *Mtsyri, Pan,* and especially *The Scythians.* The only published works are songs, some of them German in character and not very original (the composer was partly educated in Germany, and all his early works, we are told, show signs of the influence he underwent there), others —notably the three of op. 10, one of them a charming *Bear-Cub's Lullaby*—are racy and original.

Nikolai Tcherepnin (*b.* 1873) at the outset of his career was influenced by both Rimsky-Korsakof and Tchaikovsky; and later (not obtrusively) by modern French music. He is gifted with taste, feeling, and flexibility of technique and outlook. His ballets *Le Pavillon d'Armide, The Masque of the Red Death, Dionysios,* and *Russian Fairy-Tales* are the most important part of his output, which also includes symphonies, tone-poems, a sinfonietta in memory of Rimsky-Korsakof, songs, and church-music.

George Catoire (1861–1926) is regarded in Russia, jointly with Liadof, as a link between the nineteenth-century nationalists and the tendencies that asserted themselves after 1918—a view for which it is difficult to find cogent reasons, but which there is no definite reason for rejecting. His music is attractive, and testifies to a fine sense of texture. The list of his works includes a symphony, a tone-poem, *Mtsyri*, concertos, chamber-music, choral music, piano music, and songs.

Edwin Evans, in Cobbett's *Cyclopedic Survey*, calls attention to the number of second-rank Russian composers who were Rimsky-Korsakof's pupils, and whose music, although opening no new vistas, is pleasant to play and to hear. One is Nikolai Sokolof (1859–1922), whose principal compositions are three string quartets, a string trio, a ballet, *The Wild Swans*, and incidental music for Shakespeare's *A Winter's Tale*. One of his most attractive works is the Scherzo on Breton folk-tunes in *Les Vendredis*.

Les Vendredis are a set of pieces for string quartet, by various composers, written for performance at the musical evenings in the home of Belaief, the publisher. It includes the lovely Scherzo in quintuple time by Borodin afterwards transferred to his (unfinished) third Symphony. Other sets composed for the same purpose are the *Quatuor B-la-F*, in four movements by Rimsky-Korsakof, Liadof, Borodin, and Glazunof respectively, Borodin's contribution being a delightful little Serenade; the *Quatuor Jour de Fête* (intended for Belaief's name-day), in three movements by Glazunof, Liadof, and Rimsky-Korsakof, the first two being excellent examples of archaic vernacular style; and *Variations on a Russian Theme*, by twelve composers—a very mixed lot.

Other cases in point are to be found in Ivan Kryjanovsky (1867–1924) and Vassili Zolotaref (*b.* 1873). The former is at his best in his songs and chamber-music, which are poetic and expressive, although devoid of originality. His other principal works are a piano and a violin concerto, organ music, a cantata, *Paradise and the Peri*, and orchestral music, most of it unpublished. Zolotaref is more imaginative and powerful. He has to his credit a fair quantity of attractive chamber-music (four string quartets, a string quartet, a piano quartet, and a piano trio), a symphony, and a Hebrew Rhapsody for orchestra, songs, and piano music.

Felix Blumenfeld (1863–1931) deserves to be remembered not so much for his few contributions to the repertory of orchestral and chamber-music as for his songs, many of which are genuinely poetic, and his piano music, which is far less known than it deserves to be. His numerous Preludes, Études, and Lyrical Pieces ought to find a place beside Rachmaninof's. Sigismund Blumenfeld, his brother, is of lesser account.

Others, who started their career at the same period, but came to the fore mainly after 1918, will be considered in later chapters, but two more should be mentioned here. Viatcheslav Karatyghin

(1875-1925), mainly known as a critic and scholar, has composed a small number of attractive songs, mainly about children. Nikolai Lodyjensky (1843-1916) was one of Balakiref's most gifted pupils, but in the 'seventies had to give up composition owing to the exigencies of his diplomatic career. Only a few songs of his are published. They testify to a rare capacity for melodic and harmonic invention and to far-reaching poetic feeling. They remain unknown outside Russia.

CHAPTER XII

THE NON-NATIONALISTS

WE have now passed the point at which the nationalist movement began to subside. "Every achievement of genius", a French critic said, "is bound to create a conventionalism." But, although a routine of composing on national lines was bound to develop in the wake of the masters whose works we have been considering, and to become, exactly as did the academic routine, a matter of surface aspects, a lure for weaklings and hangers-on, it need not have happened thus. The nationalist innovations were not in the least incompatible with the great tradition of Western music understood in the right spirit. In many respects, the music of Debussy, Ravel, Bartók, and Kodaly represents further advance in the very direction taken by the great Russians. Had similarly minded composers of genius arisen in Russia, the evolution would have continued in that country too. Indeed, Stravinsky, in his early stages, proceeded on genuinely vernacular lines: but later, as already mentioned (p. 14), he took a different direction. The curve of his evolution after 1918 is, in the main, not dissimilar to that of Glazunof.

We have seen that another cause was the self-consciousness of certain composers who felt they lacked technical ability, and, longing to emulate their Western colleagues on their own ground, developed a mistrust of nationalism almost equal to Anton Rubinstein's.

The non-nationalist movement, it is true, had a bad start, for the reason that Anton Rubinstein (1830–1894), its leader, lacked, as a composer, the divine spark. "He was", Cesar Cui wrote, "a composer of talent—of far greater talent than is revealed in his works." The verdict is sound, so long as we realize that his talent resided exclusively in his capacity to assimilate the conventionalisms of Western music. He had great technical skill, but no creative imagination whatsoever. Except for a few minor works, his enormous output has sunk into oblivion.

With the coming of Serghei Taneief (1856–1915) and Nikolai Medtner (b. 1879), the non-nationalist Russian school became worthy of notice. If these two, and others who will be mentioned presently, may be described as musically non-Russian, it is not because they strove to acquire skill and knowledge by studying the technique and methods of Western art, but because they did not apply such skill and knowledge as they acquired to solving the problems of vernacular music. Even more than Glazunof, Taneief was an expert contrapuntist, who, had he been so minded, could well have contributed to evolving a new contrapuntal style based on the rude, racy polyphony of Russian folk-song. He did, at one time, experiment in treating vernacular tunes contrapuntally. But the central problem, for him, as for Medtner, was to keep to Western usage in all its purity, and steer clear of anything that might smack of vernacular innovations and all innovations on unconventional lines.

Arthur Symons, in an Essay on Watts, remarks:

> There is a profound kind of originality, which becomes so by its very refusal to take any of the obvious roads to that end. . . . The spirit of the man pervades his work with a kind of abnegation, resolute to speak the language of great art, and that language only, no matter who may have spoken it before.

The difficulty for the critic lies in seeing the essential beneath the obvious. With the nationalists, it is the non-observance of certain conventions that is the obvious, and the critic's task is to decide if this helped to fulfil a genuine artistic purpose. With the non-nationalists, the obvious is the conventionality, and the critic has to decide whether they give us genuine eloquence, or only rhetoric derived from the eloquence of their great predecessors. A long book would be required to consider the countless aspects of the problem of originality, and the mixture of truth and fallacy that underlies even the most plausible definitions of the term.

But, even so, it should be clear enough that to describe a group of Russian composers as non-nationalists is definition, not disparagement. It covers the fact that their idiom, syntax, and methods do not raise the same special, and at times controversial, questions as those of the nationalists. It should tempt no commentator to emulate the arrogance that conventionally-minded critics show when judging Balakiref, Borodin, and Mussorgsky.

A few remarks of Prof. Alfred J. Swan's in an essay on Medtner (*Music and Letters*, Jan. 1927) will suffice to illustrate the point: Medtner, he says, always aims at perfectly symmetrical balance. He uses no modal scales; he keeps to regular, formal methods of modulation, hardly ever resorting to enharmony, to modern harmonies, or to so-called impressionistic colour effects. Although he occasionally uses asymmetric time-signatures ($\frac{5}{4}$, $\frac{7}{4}$, etc.), he hardly ever introduces a change of time in the course of a piece.

Remembering that he is of German blood, although Russian-born, one is not surprised to feel that the German classical idiom is the natural vehicle of his musical thought, and that he could no more have felt at home in the Russian vernacular than Borodin or Mussorgsky in the idiom of Brahms and Reger. From the very outset he has shown a remarkable consistency and singleness of purpose; and he is never to be seen fluctuating, as are Tchaikovsky and Rachmaninof. A critic once remarked that he composed in a German, nineteenth-century sort of way. Not only his idiom, methods, colour-range, and tone, but also his dreaminess, his poetic feeling, his capacity for losing himself in meditation, are typically German and conservative. He is as much a dreamer as a formalist, and it is when he dreams that he is at his most imaginative. His output consists chiefly of piano music, of which a large proportion will repay study—notably the *Skazkas* (Legends), some thirty in number, the *Novellen*, the three sets of *Forgotten Melodies*, and the Sonatas. The second of his violin sonatas is the best of his few ventures into the province of chamber-music. His songs are but moderately characteristic at best. He has composed three piano concertos.

Taneief's abhorrence of modern devices was even greater than Medtner's, and his conception of music was a strictly intellectual one. Early in his career he developed a passion for strict counterpoint; and gradually, he mastered all the secrets of contrapuntal technique. He had no great gift of melodic invention. Even in his chamber-music (which is the biggest part of his output, and, with his two cantatas *St. John of Damascus* and *On the Reading of a Psalm* and a small amount of choral music, the most representative), the themes and melodies are, for the most part, of mediocre value. But he commands the art of getting the utmost out of them. Rimsky-Korsakof has recorded that before beginning the composition of a work, he devoted much time to experimenting with the themes he had selected for it, writing canons and fugues on them, cutting them up into their tiniest components, and submitting each of these to elaborate polyphonic treatment. This procedure he followed even when engaged on composing the *Oresteia*, his one and only contribution to the operatic repertory. " One might think ", Rimsky-Korsakof remarks, " that the outcome would be dry and academic: but on the contrary the music, for all its premeditation, proved to be most beautiful and expressive "—an opinion that to the present day remains that of a very small minority.

His chamber-music has not made much headway—not even the fourth and sixth string quartets and the piano quintet, which are generally regarded as his best. His songs—most of them conventional, and decidedly German in character—are fairly well known. His orchestral output includes four symphonies, two of which are unpublished.

Two pupils of Taneief may be mentioned here. Paul Juon (1872–1940; his family was of Swiss origin, but long settled in Russia) was educated partly in Moscow, partly in Berlin, where he spent the greater part of his life. He has composed a good deal of chamber-music for various combinations, a few orchestral works, including two violin concertos, piano music, songs, and a ballet, *Psyche*. He often used Russian elements, but his methods of treatment were cosmopolitan, and mainly German.[1] His technique is supple and versatile. George Conus (1862–1933) was an able but unoriginal craftsman, who made his mark chiefly as a theorist and educator. His output includes a ballet, a couple of tone-poems, piano music, and songs.

Jointly with them, Alexander Gödicke (*b.* 1877) should be considered. He has to his credit, among other things, three symphonies (which competent Russian critics have praised), an opera, and a few chamber works, the most important of which is a piano quintet. He is classically inclined, and his music, in style and spirit, stands close to Medtner's.

The fundamental difference between Alexander Scriabin (1872–1915) and the other non-nationalists of the period is that whereas their orientation was determined by a desire to keep to the old classical tradition and to speak the language of great art, his ambitions were of an egregious and non-traditional order, especially from the moment when he started dreaming of achieving something quite apart, unique, and never dreamt of before—a synthesis of all the arts, in which music would be, not an end in itself, but only one of many means of inducing an ecstatic (or perhaps it would be more accurate to say a hysterical) state. The final goal was to be the *Mystery*, in which music, dancing, poetry, colour effects, and perfumes would co-operate.

He was endowed with deftness and feeling for music rather than with creative imagination. His piano compositions on a small scale (*e.g.*, some of his Preludes and Études) contain the best music he was capable of turning out—music whose style is unblushingly but skilfully imitated from Chopin's and Wagner's. In order to cope with his colossal scheme, he devised an entirely manufactured idiom and resorted to all manners of artifices, all based on a " synthetic chord " of seven arbitrarily selected notes. Most of the

[1] See, in Cobbett's *Cyclopedic Survey of Chamber Music*, an excellent article on his chamber-music by E. Evans.

works he composed from 1900 onwards are steps towards the building up of approaches to the *Mystery*. The finale of the third piano sonata, for instance, aims at evoking, Scriabin himself said: " The intoxicated Soul striving and wrestling in the storm of the unchained elements. From the depths of its being, the voice of the Man-God arises, singing a song of victory. . . ." But it is especially with three big orchestral works, *Le Divin Poème*, *Le Poème de l'Extase*, and *Prométhée : le Poème du Feu*, that he won adherents ready to accept him at his own valuation, not only among the more gullible or excitable members of the public at large, but also among the experienced and fastidious. Ernest Newman, for instance, wrote, after the first London performance of *Prometheus*:

> Here is music that comes as near as is at present possible to being the pure voice of Nature and the soul themselves . . . the wind that blows through it is the veritable wind of the cosmos itself. The cries of desire and passion and ecstasy are a sort of quintessential sublimation of all the yearning, not merely of humanity, but of all nature, animate and inanimate. (Quoted by Cecil Gray in *A Survey of Contemporary Music*.)

Diffused in many countries, mainly by two distinguished Russian conductors, Ziloti and Kussevitsky, they enjoyed a more or less widespread appreciation for a period. " That they should have succeeded in imposing themselves on the public and maintaining their hold on it for so long is one of the most inexplicable aberrations in the chequered history of art ", Gray continues; and he ascribes the strength and longevity of the craze to the fact that " Scriabin gave us synthetic music, a product which bears much the same relation to music as saccharine to sugar, or cultured pearls to real pearls. It satisfies triumphantly all the more mechanical tests of criticism. It has all the appearance of art. Everything is there except the vital principle." But another reason, adduced in *The Outlook* by the reviewer of a book on Scriabin published in 1923, was that " many people, through sheer indolence, had conceded the full claims of the Scriabinists, and allowed to the composer a position absurdly out of place with his merits ". Gray, too, notes that for quite a long time there was no active opposition to his music. This is not altogether surprising. In those days, most of the critics and music-lovers who, by nature or by virtue of their musical experiences, were best qualified to see through Scriabin, had more important claims on their time and labour. Much of the best nineteenth-century Russian music was insufficiently known. Mussorgsky's works had to be rescued from oblivion, those of

Debussy, Ravel, Fauré, Bartok, Stravinsky, and others to be critically assessed. In 1912 or so, the Schönberg problem began to loom large. Possibly most of those whom such matters interested never noticed the spread of the Scriabin cult; or, if they did, failed to deem it necessary to expend energies on opposing it. After 1918, the number of more urgent tasks grew even greater; and it was becoming obvious that a reaction was setting in. By now, it seems more than likely that no new wave of uncritical Scriabinism will spread.[1]

Vladimir Rebikof (1866–1920), an industrious and sincere composer, but one whose methods are wholly derivative, and amateurish at best, started in the wake of romanticism—e.g., with his *Tableaux Musicaux-Psychologiques* for piano, *Aspirer et Atteindre*, *Esclavage et Liberté*, and so on, and continued in the wake of the modernists, dabbling in recent innovations such as the whole-tone scale, chords in fourths, unresolved discords generally, and so on. By a curious aberration, Sabaneief represents him as anticipating the very composers whose example, in actual fact, he followed; and this mistake has spread from the dictionary articles in which it was committed.

Rebikof has composed, among other things, operas, minor musical plays, church music, and a good deal of piano music. In his vocal compositions, and especially his songs, the influence of Mussorgsky is felt at times, making for a measure of vernacular character. His settings of fables by Krylof are cases in point.

[1] For more circumstantial particulars of Scriabin and his works, consult: (1) *Pro*: Sabaneief's and Swan's books on Scriabin (both 1923); (2) *Contra*: Gray's *Survey*, from which only greatly abridged quotations are given here.

CHAPTER XIII

STRAVINSKY, PROKOFIEF

FOR close upon a third of a century, controversy has been raging on the subject of Igor Stravinsky's music; not even Schönberg's has given rise to a greater spate of praise and denunciations.

His first big works, the ballets *The Fire-Bird* (1910), *Petrushka* (1911), and *The Rite of Spring* (1913) came at a time when the national movement was dying out for lack of a composer of genius to carry it further. And for a while it seemed that with his advent, that movement was to be given a new lease of life. All three works were thoroughly in the national tradition from all points of view, although with one difference. They testified to wonderful gifts, the only weak point being the scope and quality of the melodic invention; to an extraordinary surety of purpose and execution; and to that consummate mastery in craftsmanship and, so to speak, musical strategy which he continued to display throughout the further, often disconcerting stages of his career. And, above all, they were original, stimulating, live.

The difference was that Stravinsky, Russian born and educated in Russia, had come very much under the influence of the French composers, who, as explained in Chapter IV, had benefited by the earlier Russians' innovations. He is to be regarded as proceeding not only from Glinka, Borodin, and Rimsky-Korsakof, but from Debussy, Dukas, and Ravel.

Thence, in his music, a number of style-features not to be encountered in that of his Russian forbears, but re-incorporated into the musical language of Russia after having undergone transmutations abroad. This difference is to be felt even in *The Fire-Bird*, a ballet version of a typically Russian folk-tale. Stravinsky, in the main, keeps close to the ways of the picturesque, decorative, fantastic music of Glinka, Rimsky-Korsakof, and Liadof, but goes much farther in textual elaboration, play of rhythms, harmonies, and colours.

In *Petrushka*, the principal characters are puppets—Petrushka, a Ballerina, and a Blackamoor—exhibited at a fair by their magician owner. The crowd scenes are pure vernacular, akin to the similar scenes, previously mentioned, in Rimsky-Korsakof's operas. But the music of the Petrushka, Ballerina, and Blackamoor scenes is of a far more distinctive and subtler order, and belongs to Stravinsky's best. By means of countless sharp, deft touches, he manages not only to achieve a high degree of pantomimic characterization, but to convey, in elusive yet unmistakable ways, a feeling of the strange mixture of high-grade puppetry and primitive humanity that they constitute.

The Rite of Spring evokes prehistoric Russia. In 1913 the harshness and violence of the music left even experienced and unprejudiced listeners aghast. Paul Claudel described it as " so cruel that it attacked the soul as an icy north wind or a merciless sun the body ". Its physical effectiveness is amazing. It acts by sheer force and insistence. It does not aim at appealing to any definable kind of human emotion, nor to poetic imagination, nor to the intellect. It must be " yielded to " rather than " grasped "; and maybe the best way to listen to it is to listen passively—the very worst way, as a rule, of listening to music worth listening to. But, then, *The Rite of Spring* is, for this and other reasons, in a class by itself, and a kind of thing that could not be done twice. Stravinsky, realizing as much, refrained from attempting a second experiment on similar lines.

His further course almost suggests that the very thoroughness of his achievement in those three works gave rise to satiety and disenchantment. He gradually progressed towards an ideal that can be defined as the elimination from his music of all that struck him as unessential or out of place, beginning with expression. He developed remarkable notions as to the function of music. Every now and again, declarations of his, written or verbal, made clear his attitude of the moment to his art; and it is impossible to deal with the series of his works without referring to them.

As early as 1909, while working on his opera *The Nightingale*, he had begun to feel that " he could write music to words or music to action, but that the co-operation of music with both words and action was daily becoming more inadmissible to his mind "; and that even should he finish *The Nightingale,* he would probably never again undertake a work of that kind.[1] And, in effect, the only other opera he turned out afterwards was *Mavra*, a short affair of the opera buffa order. But in those days he steadfastly believed in the expressive power of music: " I always aim at straightforward expression in its simplest form. I have no use for working out in dramatic or in lyric music. The one essential thing is to feel and to convey one's feelings " (*ib.*). How far away from this simple, and in form almost Mussorgsky-like attitude, his speculations

[1] Sayings recorded by the present writer in the *Musical Times*, June 1914.

eventually led him is shown by the following lines in his *Memoirs*
(1935):

> I hold music to be essentially powerless to express anything
> whatsoever, be it a feeling, an attitude, a state of mind, or a
> natural phenomenon. Expression never was an immanent
> property of music. If music seems to express something, this
> is merely an illusion, an added element with which a tacit
> inveterate convention credits it.

As Ansermet, the distinguished conductor, puts it in one of his
many essays on Stravinsky, these views may be accounted for by
the fact that Stravinsky is, first to last, an artisan, who believes that
beauty lies in his materials and craftsmanship, and is best brought
out by the artist's concentrating on his craft in a practical, impersonal
spirit. He probably is the most enquiring composer of to-day, and
certainly the most restless. During the 'twenties and 'thirties, he
kept constantly experimenting in some direction or other. He
turned *The Nightingale* first into a ballet and later into a tone-poem.
He explored all conceivable methods of eliminating expression.
In the *Symphonies for Wind Instruments* (1920) all the instruments
have to play in their natural *mezzo-forte* throughout, without the
slightest change. Expressive changes of tempo are banned, and
performers instructed to do nothing but play the notes exactly as
written.

Elsewhere, the strings, or part of them, are eliminated as too
expressive. *Les Noces*, a very fine choral ballet (1917), the only
work in which, after the *Rite of Spring*, he reverted to the national
vernacular idiom, is set for percussion instruments and four pianos.
For the opera oratorio *Œdipus Rex* (1927) he used a text written in
Latin, the language being selected on account of its " remote and
petrified quality ". The principal actors remain encased in stiff
costumes and masks; they move only their hands and heads, and
must have the appearance of living statues. A speaker in evening
suit comes to the proscenium to explain the action.

While proceeding with unflagging assurance along his chosen
path, he kept on looking forward and around him and backwards
for new problems to solve and fresh solutions of old problems. He
turned to the territories of jazz and rag-music with *Rag-time* for
eleven instruments, *Piano-Rag-music* (1919), and especially to
musical styles of the past: to that of Handel in *Œdipus Rex*, that
of Bach in the Piano Concerto (1924), that of Lully in *Apollo
Musagetes* (1927), that of Tchaikovsky in the little opera-buffa

Mavra (1922). His ballet *Pulcinella* (1920) is partly based on sonatas by Pergolesi.

While experimenting thus, he strove towards increasing sobriety of means, towards music increasingly austere and unadorned as well in its moods of fun as in its most earnest moods. On the other hand, he tried to compensate for this parsimony by introducing other elements of interest, aiming above all at sharpness of definition and pungency of rhythms and colours.

One of the most surprising things about the output of all those years is that it should contain nothing that proved surprising in the same way as the *Rite of Spring* or the *Symphonies for Wind Instruments* had proved to be in their time. What is disconcerting is that they should be so very much simpler; that he should be so anxious, not only to restrict the range of his vocabulary, but to pin his faith on hackneyed, and, as often as not, fundamentally commonplace ideas and processes.

Several English critics have expressed a similar view; for instance, W. R. Anderson (*Musical Times*, March 1936), with reference to *Œdipus Rex*:

> Once again we pondered the problem of Stravinsky in Search of a Style. He is the Flying Dutchman of music: he seeks salvation and goes to and fro in the earth, and will not give up . . . will he ever find salvation?

All this was bewildering, no doubt; and gave rise to much adverse criticism. "Stravinsky's story", the French critic Léon Vallas wrote in 1929, "is very similar to his own *Histoire du Soldat*, the story of the poor soldier forever trudging, ever believing he is trudging forward, and, in order to create the illusion of a continuous advance, compelled, now to mark time, now to go round in circles, making much ado about nothing, discovering things universally known, and beginning afresh, with all the ardour of a neophyte, experiments that have been carried out for centuries, and long since given up by others."

Stravinsky's reply to his critics, in his *Memoirs*, is:

> I clearly feel that with the works I turned out after 1920 I part company with the majority of my public. Other things had been expected from me. Loving *The Fire-Bird*, *Petrushka*, *The Rite*, and *Noces*, and being accustomed to the language I use in those works, they are astonished to hear me using another. They cannot or will not follow the progress of my musical thinking. That which moves me and gives me joy leaves them

cold, that which continues to interest them attracts me no longer. My recent works find favour with a number of the younger people. Maybe it is all a question of generation. No wonder that our Aristarchs should be confused by music that does not conform to their æsthetics. But why should they condemn what they simply fail to understand? They certainly shall not deflect me from the path I chose.

Many of the critics who studied Stravinsky's course most carefully aver that even in those works of his that appear to be most derivative, and made of commonplaces, he is thoroughly himself, and always the same. Thus, notably, André Schaeffner in his excellent book on Stravinsky (Paris, 1931). The Russian critic Boris de Schloezer expresses the same view, but with an important qualification:

> Usually, when dealing with a work by a great composer we find out that it is more or less related to his past works and conduces to his later works. But it seems as though this was not the case with Stravinsky's output; that except for his latest works, no two of them have anything in common—that each of them is conditioned either by his *hoc volo, sic jubeo* or by external circumstances. Nevertheless, there is a certain unity in this output—a unity which depends on consistency not of technique or idiom, but of purpose. Stravinsky has always a definite purpose, and always selects the most suitable means of achieving it. His many changes of front are manifestations of a consistent tendency. His art is not in the least revolutionary. He tries not to break loose from tradition, but to go deeper within its bounds. Again, those changes of his take place on a purely æsthetic plane; his human personality is never involved. This means that as an artist he is altogether free, but within certain limits. Creative power does not consist of culture only, and even culture cannot live forever on its own reserves: contact with psychological, social, and religious reality, fresh experiences of life are necessary. Stravinsky's art, which after all is in itself but a secondary, artificial phenomenon, is in danger of sinking into mere academism and stylization. In *Le Baiser de la Fée*, in the *Symphonie de Psaumes*, the *Duo Concertant* and the Violin Concerto, processes and formulæ begin to stand out. This is why a reaction against Stravinsky has started, in the name of frank, straightforward, human expression.

(*Rassegna Musicale*, March 1934.)

But, truth to tell, some of his published declarations are the reverse of helpful from the music-lover's point of view, however instructive historians may find them. One of the most curious is that which heralded the production of his choreographic drama *Persephone* in 1934:

> I do not exteriorize. I hold that music is given us to create order, to carry us from an anarchical, individual condition to a regulated condition, thoroughly conscious and provided with guarantees of enduring vitality. That which specifically appertains to my conscious emotion cannot be expressed in regulated form. When emotion becomes conscious, it is already cold and set. . . . I warn the public, that I loathe orchestral effects as means of embellishment. I have long since renounced the futilities of *brio*. I dislike cajoling the public: . . . The crowd expects the artist to tear out his own entrails and exhibit them. That is what is held to be the noblest expression of art, and called personality, individuality, temperament, and so on. . . . This score, as it is written and as it must remain in the archives of our time, forms an indiscerptible whole with the tendencies repeatedly asserted in my previous works.
>
> It is a sequel to *Œdipus Rex*, to the *Symphonie de Psaumes*, to the *Capriccio*, to the Violin Concerto, and to the *Duo Concertant*—in short, to a progression from which the spectacular is absent without this absence affecting the autonomous life of the works. . . . Nothing of all this originates in a caprice of my own. I am on a perfectly sure road. There is nothing to discuss nor to criticize. One does not criticize anybody or anything that is functioning. A nose is not manufactured: a nose just *is*. Thus, too, my art.

The idea expressed in the last lines might have been formulated no less justifiably (or, should one not say, no less unjustifiably?) by any composer, and in respect of any work, from *Parsifal* to *Pagliacci*. What is amazing is that the one who formulated it should be he who, a bare twelvemonth later, declared, in his Memoirs, that " the spectator's attitude is determined neither by faith nor by blind submission. He either admires or rejects: and this entails a judgment, an operation of the critical faculty, which faculty plays an all-essential part."

To make a long story short: it remains true that every one of his later works has found a measure of warm support, and also, that some of them have been praised in strikingly reluctant terms.

Thus G. Pannain on *Œdipus Rex* (in *Modern Composers*, London, 1934)':

> He has substituted a semblance for the real soul, and imagines he has created a new and boundless world. He wrote *Œdipus* in a spirit of sackcloth and ashes. . . . He has put himself in a prison, but his nature reacts against the self-donned fetters, and succeeds in producing a work with elements of grandeur and power.

Likewise Cortot, in an essay on his piano music:

> In many of his works, the piano acquires an aspect of inclement beauty of which no musician had ever caught a glimpse so far. We can but respect the courage with which, obeying the dictates of his conscience, he pursues his lonely march towards the unknown horizon peopled with grim enchantments, the creations of his cold-blooded intellectuality.

In fine, whether one belongs to the considerable majority of those who prefer his early works to those that came after 1918, and whether one inclines or not to endorse the view, expressed by many of his admirers, that all his changes of purpose, style, and methods are but the natural and logical outcome of 'one consistent and unswerving artistic policy, one is likely to agree with Eric Blom's conclusion (in Grove's *Dictionary*) that even his latest ventures show " a keenly intelligent artist still at work upon an unceasing quest after new ways and means of expression, and ever intent on achieving the utmost virtuosity of craftsmanship ".

Serghei Prokofièf (*b.* 1891) is in most respects the very antithesis of Stravinsky: carefree, impulsive, never concerned with abstractions. Nor are the style and character of his music ever determined by any preconceived notion of what music ought or ought not to be. He started composing early. By the time he was twenty, he had turned out a considerable amount of piano music, a symphonietta (1909, revised 1926), a piano concerto, and two little operas, only one of which is preserved. The first works of his to attract attention outside Russia were the ballet *Chout* (Buffoon) and the comic opera *The Love for the Three Oranges*, both produced in 1921, the former in Paris and the latter in Chicago.

These two brilliantly farcical works, coming at so short an interval from a composer not yet widely known to the public, earned for him the reputation of an irrepressible jester. The boldness and whimsicality of his experiments in idiom and colour confirmed it. And so, people began to think of him as the *enfant terrible* of Russian music—an ill-advised label, which, besides leaving out of count his serious works, does not do justice to the genuineness and wealth of his musical imagination, to the splendidly workmanlike quality of his technique—in short, to all that is the real Prokofief, the very antipode of a musical scapegrace even in his most exuberantly humorous or remorselessly satirical moods.

The truth is that, endowed with a mind no less enquiring than Stravinsky's, he started by experimenting in many directions, from the systematic yet unlaboured bitonality that crops up, for instance, in his *Sarcasms* for piano and his Sonata op. 38, to the deliberate adoption, in his *Symphonie Classique* and other works, earlier or later, of the forms and idiom of the pre-Beethoven Viennese period— a step with which, it may be said, he foreshadowed Stravinsky's " returns " to old classical usage.

Maybe the Russian critic Sabaneief is right in saying that humorous moods are disproportionately prevalent in his works. Still, the spirit of musical fun is an important element in his personality, and it would have been a great pity if he had not given it full play. There exists all too little genuinely and intrinsically farcical music; and of that little too large a proportion is of a commonplace, stereotyped order—the musical equivalent of the plumber's-mate or cold-feet jokes. Prokofief often gives us what few others, if any, could give. In *Chout* the farce on the stage often becomes horseplay pure and simple: but the music never. The angularity, acidity, and harshness, the touches of garishness which render the colour-scheme comparable, in many ways, to what we find in the native art of Russia's peasantry, are part of a well-thought-out and cleverly carried out scheme. The story of *The Love for the Three Oranges* is as irresponsible—but by no means as subtle—as *Alice in Wonderland*. It lacks the essential virtues of *Alice*; it cannot be accepted even as convincing make-believe. There is no appeal to human nature or human reason in it, and not even the logic of topsy-turvydom is called into play: but the music vivifies it, so that we enter the spirit of the thing and take it all in our stride.

He shows the same efficiency in his works of the earnest order. It has often been said that his music lacks under-currents; that, as another Russian critic put it, round about 1933 (the reason for calling attention to that date will presently appear), " there is no trace in it of that idea-contents which we regard as a · necessary condition of the greatest art ". And for that reason, although it can be, and generally is, entertaining and interesting in many respects, it is hardly ever companionable. His chief concern, during all that period, was to concentrate upon the possibilities of the materials of music, which fascinated him far more than the philosophical purport of the results he achieved.

The way in which he manœuvred notes and patterns, toying with chords and rhythms, revelling in the fun of repeating and prolonging and contrasting and interrupting (many of his works contain long passages that seem to have been written with the object of finding out all that can be done with and around one note) showed that his interest went, not, like Stravinsky's, to the objective abstractions of form and volume, but to the tangible realities of tone and rhythm, shunning neither complications nor simplicity, neither expression nor pure pattern-play. His way of carrying on may appear, now and then, rather rough; sometimes a trifle wilful, yet it is orderly enough, and well kept within bounds. Everything is as carefully calculated as can be, but never on the basis of a preconceived theory.

The list of his works up to 1934 includes five piano concertos, one violin concerto, four symphonies, a *Scythian Suite* for orchestra, the operas *The Gambler* and *The Flaming Angel*, and several ballets. The piano concertos, especially the third, are a very characteristic part of his output. The *Scythian Suite* is one of his best works, robust and exhilarating—the only one, apart from his Russian Overture of 1936, in which he resorted extensively to vernacular elements—but vernacular, as with Stravinsky, at the second remove.

It is interesting to note that while he appeared truest to his nature when revelling in vivid colours, and strong flavours, the inclination to simplicity was gaining ground within him. It made itself felt especially in his ballet *The Prodigal Son* (1928), a quintet for wind and strings (1923), and an *Overture on Jewish Themes* for piano, string quartet, and clarinet, which belong to his best. In the one and only profession of faith he ever gave out (in 1936; issued to the Press by Opera Mundi) he referred to this stage of his evolution as follows:

In my youth, I sought above all things to compose original, singular music. Later, I began to delve deeper below the surface of the art. I started going in for simplicity immediately after having composed my second and third symphonies, in which I indulged in complex artifices. My three piano sonatinas were the first-fruit of this policy. At that time [N.B.: the middle twenties] the quest for novelty had led to such excesses that a reaction was bound to follow, a number of composers seeking to discover a simple, clear language—which of course had to be thoroughly novel under pain of being meaningless. Certain people are ever urging me to go in for feeling, for emotion, for melody. And so I do, but they are unable to realize it. Maybe, because of the novelty of my melodies, I am striving to discover new melodies, based on new patterns, and not to pour new wine into old bottles. Not all ears are equally capable of perceiving melodies that are new.

In 1934 Prokofief, who since 1917 had been working abroad (in the U.S.A., and later in France), decided to return to Russia and settle there. At that time, as will be explained in the next chapter, the Soviet authorities were very much concerned with ensuring that musical art should conform to Marxist ideology, that music should be simple enough to prove accessible and intelligible to all, and be of immediate practical value from the point of view of Soviet influence and culture, a *sine qua non* being that it should steer clear of introspection and dissolving emotions, and embody active, stimulating moods.

So Prokofief found in the new Russia every incentive to persist in his policy of simplification. Of the works he composed from that time on (they include incidental music to Pushkin's *Eugen Onieghin* and *Boris Godunof*, and an *Overture on Russian Themes*) only a few have reached us. One of the best is the music for the film *Alexander Nevsky*.

CHAPTER XIV

MUSIC UNDER THE SOVIETS

With the advent, after the 1917 revolution, of the Soviet régime, conditions underwent radical alterations; and the changes resulting from the tremendous upheaval deeply affected the course of music, as well as that of all the other arts. Confronted with the task of evolving a new order from principles rather than from experience, everyone started casting about for solutions of problems not always clearly formulated. Education (including artistic education) for the masses was one of the new Government's chief concerns, another being the immediate practical part that the arts could play in the matter of Soviet influence and culture.

This led to the social and moral aspects of music being given precedence over the purely æsthetic, with the ultimate consequence that, for the first time in the world's history, musical art was drawn into the direct service of State policy and expected to contribute positive help in furthering this policy's aims; and accordingly, was hemmed in by prescriptions and restrictions which composers were compelled to obey.

This happened not all of a sudden, but by degrees. As early as 1918, it is true, a Musical Department of the Ministry of Education was founded, its head being, until 1931, Arthur Lourié, an alert and cultured young composer who had, it would seem, no axe of his own, either political or æsthetic, to grind. But, as Lourié himself pointed out (in the *Musical Quarterly*, October 1932):

> In the early days of the upheaval, there was no contact between art and politics. During that period, art occupied an aristocratic, privileged position. The musical life of Russia was restricted to its professionals. Musical creation continued to use its own æsthetic processes. The political workers were not concerned with music, and the musicians shut their eyes to politics and tried to maintain the " art for art's sake " position, which was essentially a thing of the past. Later on, when a cultural front was announced, the drama, literature and painting were brought into contact with the Marxist doctrine far more quickly than music.

Naturally enough, literature and the drama were the first to be pressed into service: but this happened mainly because of the zeal of volunteer groups and organizations such as the " Proletcult ", all eager to ensure supplies of the right kind of literature for the masses.[1]   The results were such that in 1922, when the New Econo- mic Policy came into being, a resolution was passed that " The Party should fight against all thoughtless and contemptuous treat- ment of the old cultural heritage and of literary specialists, and also against a purely hot-house proletarian literature."

In 1928 a Russian Association of Proletarian Writers was founded, with the consequence that for a time writers who did not declare their absolute devotion to communism were the objects of envenomed attacks, and reviews and publishing houses were shut against them. One of the outstanding features of the early years of the first Five- Year Plan was the summons into literature of 10,000 *Udarniki* (shock brigade workers) and peasants who had shown some literary inclinations, in order to replenish the ranks of Soviet literature and endow it with a really proletarian spirit.   It was soon felt that the Association was doing more harm than good.   In 1931 a decree ordered its dissolution.

Practically the same thing happened with music: but far more complex a situation had to be faced.   It is easy enough, when all is said and done, to determine the ideology—or, to put it more accurately, the idea-contents—of even the most cryptic, elliptical, and ambitiously stylized literary text: but not so with music, as was demonstrated for the *n*th time when the problem came to be tackled in Soviet Russia.

Again, the Soviet Government did not forthwith take the matter in hand; but well-meaning volunteers rushed in to help lay down the new laws. In 1924 a Russian Association of Proletarian Musi- cians was founded, anticipating by four years the foundation of the Association of Proletarian Writers.   Its leaders were the composers Koval, Tchemberdji, Shekhter, Biely, and Davidenko.   Its mani- festos denounced the decay and disintegration of musical culture under *bourgeois* influences, and demanded, among other things, " the extension of the hegemony of the proletariat to the field of music, the creation of Marxist musicology and Marxist musical criticism, the creation of conditions favourable to the growth of proletarian music—music that would reflect the rich, full-blooded psychology of the proletariat, which was the most advanced, sensitive, and understanding class.   No form of contemporary *bourgeois* music that proved to be incompatible with the proletarian spirit was to be accepted.   Composers should learn from those

[1] The information provided here is taken from *Soviet Literature, an Anthology*, by G. Reavey and M. Slonim (London, 1933).

masters of the past whose music reflected proletarian ideals: Beethoven and Mussorgsky especially. All extremist innovations were to be banned."

Against this group arose, in 1929, the Association for Contemporary Music, which proclaimed that Soviet composers should learn from Central European innovators such as Alban Berg, Hindemith, Křenek, and others, whose music was full-blooded, virile, sane, and lucid, deeply emotional, and proudly restrained (documents quoted in *Sovietskaya Muzyka*, May 1936). For a time the two groups continued propagating their views, other groups joining in the fray, and a number of short-lived periodicals—*The Proletarian Musician, Music and Revolution, The New Music, Contemporary Music, Musical Culture, Musical Renovation* and others—recording the phases of the campaign.

In 1932 a State decree dissolved the Association of Proletarian Musicians, and the Union of Soviet Composers was founded. The reasons given for the dissolution were, among others, that " its theorist spokesmen, by preaching musical ignorance, strove to discredit the classical heritage, banning Chopin and Liszt, deriding Tchaikovsky, and grossly misrepresenting masters such as Beethoven and Mussorgsky, thereby doing great harm to Soviet art and Soviet musical education ".

The doctrine of the Association for Contemporary Music was not officially impugned until the beginning of 1936, when an event took place which, while severely restricting the composers' imaginative and technical scope, had the advantage of putting an end to the state of chaos brought about by the long spate of theorizing and counter-theorizing.

In 1934 an opera, *The Lady Macbeth of Mtsensk*, by Dimitri Shostakovitch (*b.* 1906), who ever since the performance in 1926 of his first symphony was generally accepted as the most brilliant exponent of Soviet music, was produced at Leningrad and hailed as a revelation, a masterpiece of high originality and power, an achievement that came close to being a perfect embodiment of Soviet musical ideals. The libretto (of which Shostakovitch was part author) was described as a ruthless and telling satire ridiculing the evils of the Tsarist régime, the cruelty and covetousness of its *bourgeois*, the stupidity and corruption of its officials, priesthood, and soldiery. The music, it was proclaimed, was not altogether free from imperfections, but stood, all told, on a very high level. None but a Soviet artist could have turned out such a work.

The opera continued its triumphant career in Russia for close upon two years. It was performed in the U.S.A., and there too received high praise. But at the beginning of 1936, Stalin and Molotof attended a performance, and decided that the work was in all respects detestable, and deserved to be banned. An article in the official *Pravda* described it as " a farrago of chaotic, nonsensical sounds, illustrating a thoroughly coarse and bestial drama, the negation of the very principles of opera and of music generally; a senseless and thoroughly non-political concoction ". The fact that it had won approval abroad, it was added, was probably due to its non-Sovietic character.

The term " non-political " is worth considering. There can be no question but that the libretto of *The Lady Macbeth* was intended as a satire of past conditions. It is based on a tale by Lieskof—the story of a woman who becomes the mistress of one of her husband's workmen, and when found out, murders her father-in-law and afterwards her husband. Lieskof had handled the grim subject with a detachment and restraint worthy of Stendhal. The librettist, on the contrary, piled up lurid and unsavoury details, distorting almost every scene and the psychology of almost every character, and introducing a number of melodramatic or crudely grotesque episodes.

But in the early days after the Revolution all lampoons against the old order were credited with some kind of propaganda value. In an earlier opera, *The Nose*, Shostakovitch had done very much the same kind of thing as in *The Lady Macbeth*, although in a more purely humorous spirit. In 1929–1930, Marian Koval, one of the leaders of the Association of Proletarian Musicians, had come forth with three operas, *The Dipsomaniac*, *The Hooligan*, and *Portrait of a Kleptomaniac*, of which no particulars are available, but which may be presumed to have struck a more or less similar note. Even later, Prokofief, in his ballet *Romeo and Juliet*, composed after he had settled down in Russia, followed the fashion by turning Friar Laurence into a Rabelaisian monk, " as was only to be expected ", a writer in *Sovietskaya Muzyka* remarked.

Eventually, a reaction set in against those facile and shallow methods of caricature. So much so that Borodin's farcical opera *The Valiant Knights*, revived in Moscow after seventy years' oblivion, with the libretto refurbished for the occasion by the Soviet poet-laureate, Biedny, had to be withdrawn by order " because in the new libretto the institutions and laws of medieval Russia were held up to ridicule ".

So far as music was concerned, the official sentence passed upon *The Lady Macbeth* (the score of which was decidedly, although not uncompromisingly, radical in character—the point will be dealt

with in the next chapter) sounded the death-knell of the views up-
held by the Association for Contemporary Music (the Association,
although not formally suppressed, ceased to exist at about the same
time).

Shostakovitch, at that point in his career, fared no better as a
composer of simple, easily accessible music. A ballet of his, *The
Limpid Brook*, an unassuming affair purporting to illustrate episodes
from life on a collective farm, was denounced in an article in *Pravda*
(February 6, 1936), entitled *Falsity in Ballet*, as being "all bogus
folk-dancing, dolled-up stage-peasantry, and bogus folk-tunes which
the composer bandied about with his tongue in his cheek", which
goes to show that whatever the leaders of Soviet opinion might
think of modern complications and excesses, they were not inclined
to abide by the loose and shallow standards that had found favour
with the Association of Proletarian Musicians. They aimed at
securing positive results.

Before proceeding farther, let us try to determine a few of the
leading ideas that stirred that world of ever-changing values, of
febrile quest for the solution of countless problems, some of them
real, others imaginary, but all of them looming large in the minds
of both artists and theorists.

The central idea is easy enough to formulate, but embodies one
of two opposite conceptions the conflict between which rages
throughout the history of musical æsthetics: on the one hand,
music as self-governed, independent of and (whatever the source of
inspiration and the composer's intentions may have been) unrelated
to anything but itself; and on the other hand, music as governed
by, and containing and expressing, something that is not "just
music"—emotions, ideas, images, symbols, and so on. In Soviet
Russia the latter conception reigns unchallenged: indeed, it is
considered that, as Shostakovitch put it in a profession of faith of
1935, "music cannot help having a political basis. There can be
no music without ideology. The old composers, whether they knew
it or not, were upholding political theories." And, moreover,
there seems to be a general agreement that, as posited by Plato in
his *Republic*, certain types of music are *per se* wholesome and bene-
ficent, others unwholesome and noxious.

"We ascribe no value", Lunacharsky, the State commissary,
proclaimed in 1933, "to any work of art—be it statue or symphony,
painting or stage-play—which does not bear some relation to the
movement that is renovating the world." One may wonder what
the relation can be when it comes to music not associated with words
or with a programme; and how, assuming it to exist, its existence
can be determined.

The question of ideology *versus* artistic value is a serious one, no doubt. One of the few indisputable principles of musical æsthetics and criticism is that, whatever view be held as to the emotional and connotative properties of music, it remains true that the higher, more developed type of listener is (to quote from W. J. Turner's *Music and Life*, London, 1921) primarily sensitive to sound and design, not to emotions, ideas, and symbols, real or imaginary. And it should be obvious that music can have no connotative properties other than such as may arise from associations bound to be the outcome, in the first instance, of accidental circumstances.[1]

The ultimate conclusion arrived at in Soviet Russia is that music should be national and full-blooded, steer clear of abstract rationalism, be simple enough in idiom and texture to be immediately accessible to the masses, intelligible even to the least alert and experienced listener.

No matter what one's own views happen to be on these points of principle, one cannot, when considering Soviet music, overlook the fact that they are accepted as the very basis of Soviet musical composition and criticism. But for them, it would be utterly impossible to account for most of the recent happenings in Soviet Russia.

The practical application of these principles proved to be no easy matter. "There existed", an editorial in *Music and Revolution* ruefully acknowledged, "no scientifically tested Marxist standards for the assessment of music." But artists and theorists worked hard to discover those elusive standards. Agreement was soon reached upon a number of general points: Soviet music was to be the embodiment of active, not of contemplative moods, introspection, emotionalism, and all "dissolving" elements being declared undesirable; non-sentimental, non-romantic, concerned with realities, and national, so as to reflect the true spirit of the people and be significant to them. Composers should aim, not at empirical representations of so-called "realistic" details, but at giving true, objective images of the world and of human feelings, at following the natural part of human thought.

On the other hand, in proportion as the investigation became more specific, there was a good deal of casting about and fumbling. Striving to determine the relations between musical processes or points of style and their psychological purport or effects, critics

---

[1] *E.g.*, the association of the opening notes of Beethoven's C minor symphony with the idea of victory, which could not have arisen but for the existence of the Morse Code as we have it; and anyhow, could not have arisen in Greece, Russia, or any country in whose language the word meaning victory does not happen to begin with the letter V.

started discussing questions such as how far horizontal, contra-puntal writing, as practised by Bach, Mahler, Reger, Hindemith, and by certain Soviet composers such as Shebalin and Shostako-vitch, was compatible with the desired realism, and whether it tended to foster a collective spirit or individualism; how a balance could be struck between the tendency to imagery and realism, which might lead to empiricism, rhetorics, and disorder, and the tendency to " pure " music, which might lead to abstraction and formalism (*Sovietskaya Muzyka*, October 1933, article by Tcheremukhin; and also *passim*).

One fine day, it was even averred that the production of symphonic music should cease, the genre not being sufficiently concrete and useful from the practical point of view (decree of April 1932). But soon afterwards, it was proclaimed that " symphony was the musical form in which the *Weltanschauung* of a period found its fullest expression "; and the fact that in other countries many of the radical, ultra-modern composers avoided tackling its problems was adduced as symptomatic.

An example or two of the judgments passed on older composers may be quoted to complete the picture. Tchaikovsky's music had been regarded for a while (in company with Chopin's, Mendelssohn's and Schumann's) as contrary to the Soviet spirit. When the verdict came to be reconsidered, it was pointed out that :

> He was the first Russian to compose symphonies whose form was determined not by picturesque imagery or impres-sions or ornamental colour schemes, but by philosophical problems conceived in the abstract. His output faithfully reflects the crisis the Russian *intelligentsia* went through during the 'eighties and after. His ideals were those of the reactionary aristocracy; and he stuck to them passionately, to the bitter end, laying bare the fundamental problem that confronted the class to which he belonged—the problem of its ultimate fate. Hence the tremendous force and the historical value of his music.

(D. Zhitomirsky in *Sovietskaya Muzyka*, December 1933.)

No less characteristic are the following lines in the poster of the Rimsky-Korsakof Exhibition organized in 1933 to commemorate the twenty-fifth anniversary of his death:

> His life and work as a whole embody the ideology of an aristocracy turned bourgeois, which believed that capitalism must unavoidably develop. Considering the way in which he

adjusted himself to the various stages of the evolution of that class, it is important for us all to study his output. The antinomies of his evolution are manifest in his fluctuations between romanticism and realism, life and history, fantasy and reality, between love of the past and pungent political satire. To become familiar with his artistic bequest, so as to achieve a critical comprehension of it, is one of the conditions of the establishment of the socialist musical culture of the revolutionary proletariat.

Russian critics and observers were not unaware of the difficulties and precariousness of it all. There was no lack of reminders that " Soviet labels did not necessarily mean Soviet contents ", that the principle that music should be accessible even to the inexperienced masses should not be allowed to foster uncritical methods and a spirit of indolence and mediocrity. How eagerly the solution of these and other similar problems was sought is shown by the many conferences and debates devoted to their investigation: for instance, " What Should Soviet Symphonism Be? " (report, 56 pages, in *Sovietskaya Muzyka*, April–June 1935); " The Moral of the Ban on *The Lady Macbeth* " (*ib.*, March 1936, 60 pages); " The Schooling and Duties of Soviet Composers " (*ib.*, May 1936, 71 pages). " Music for Children " (a particularly interesting one—*ib.*, February 1935, 73 pages). Informal meetings at which composers dissect and frankly criticize one another's works are another noteworthy feature.

On the whole, it is felt in Russia that things are moving in the right direction:

> The mental and emotional scope of Soviet creative life has considerably widened. Soviet thematism, arising from the native music of the people, has become the centre of this life, and the style of Soviet realism is taking shape.
>
> (Editorial in *Sovietskaya Muzyka*, April 1937.)

> A work such as Shostakovitch's fifth symphony could never have come into being but for the sharp, just, wise, thoroughly bolshevistic criticism in *Pravda*, by which the composer benefited.
>
> (G. Khubof, *ib.*, March 1938.)

Not all observers from abroad were equally confident; for instance, A. Clement-Marot, in the Paris *Menestrel* (March 8–15, 1940):

In the recent works of even the most gifted Soviet composers, such as Miaskovsky, Vassilenko, Prokofief, and Shostako-vitch, the preoccupation of toeing the line, of not displeasing the authorities, is ever manifest. Likewise in criticism. Meanwhile, the public remains indifferent to the new music, in which official phraseology and ideology replace artistic value.

And Gerald Abraham, in *A Hundred Years of Music* (London 1938):

> To get his work published and performed, the Soviet composer must compromise his artistic integrity and write music acceptable to the authorities. If the means is wholly bad, the end—the closing of the gulf between composer and listener—is not. The *rôle* of Marcus Curtius is not wholly unheroic.

It would be puerile to deny that there are two sides to the question. The new discipline may, up to a point, be stimulating and provide valuable guidance, but its operation seems bound to generate an atmosphere of restlessness hardly conducive to concentration and to a feeling of creative freedom. Many years ago Claude Debussy, discussing with the present writer the musical situation in Europe, said that formerly composers were allowed to mature in peace, whereas young twentieth-century artists were being unsettled through being made the subject of deplorably premature, and often shallow or prejudiced, discussion. Young Soviet composers are certainly not allowed to mature in peace. But, on the other hand, to quote information collected in Russia by Miss Evelyn Porter and published in the October 1937 *Musical Times*·

> The Union of Soviet Composers provides for the composer's material needs in congenial surroundings.
>
> The qualifications for membership of this Union are a promising talent for composition, and the intention of fostering that talent by constant work.
>
> In return the Union pays the composer a salary, and probably also pays his rent. If he is engaged on a work of some size—a symphony or an opera—the salary will continue for a period of several years if necessary. Holidays are arranged to suit the individual inclination.
>
> It is essential, they say, that a composer should have change of surroundings and experience of different peoples. Confinement to one place or one set of circumstances is not conducive to the growth of new powers of expression. Therefore it will be arranged that the composer shall make a lengthened stay in

some other part of the Soviet states.   The resulting compositions may be based on the folk-music of that state or may be
evolved from his impressions and experiences.

On completion his work is submitted to the criticism of
colleagues, and presumably altered if their opinions are unfavourable.   The Union then undertakes negotiations with the
publishing firms which collaborate with it, and makes arrangements for performance both at home and abroad.

State recognition of the value of music is shown by the fact
that next year a huge mansion, costing ten million roubles, will
be completed as the headquarters of the Union of Soviet
Composers.   An annual income of a further two or three
million roubles will be granted.

Truly, a state of things without a parallel in the history of any
art, in any civilization, and one whose ultimate consequences, by
the time it becomes possible to view them from the right distance
and in their proper perspective, will prove most instructive.   Even
now, the results are noteworthy enough.

CHAPTER XV

COMPOSERS OF SOVIET RUSSIA

Musical Russia to-day is a hive of seething ever-growing activities. Throughout the Union, composition, music-making, and the study of music are sedulously and efficiently encouraged, liberal provision being made for education and for everything that may help to foster interest in music. Consequently, a plethora of music is being turned out. Neither publishers nor producers and performers could keep pace with it, even though opportunities for performance —especially of operas, ballets, and symphonic and choral works— are many.

The task of surveying this immense field is all but impossible, considering how small a proportion of the new music is available for study. In many cases, all we have to go by is what has been said of it in the Russian Press. And that the danger of going by hearsay, serious enough always, is particularly great in the present instance is shown by what happened with Shostakovitch's *The Lady Macbeth* (see p. 101).

The years that immediately followed the Revolution were not very productive. The older men carried on as best they could. The disastrous influence of Scriabin weighed heavily upon those of the younger ones whose concern was with style and technique; those whose thinking centred on little else but the new ideology devoted their energy to turning out either elementary music for mass performance, or, as already mentioned, lampoons upon the old *régime*, or works aiming at positive propaganda of an order that P. Riazanof (discussing in *Sovietskaya Muzyka*, May 1936, the duties of Soviet composers) calls the pathetic-rhetorical—signal examples being, he says, Davidenko's opera *The Passport* (1925), Koval's *The Revolutionary Lightning* (1930), and Yudin's *The Red Rice Sways* (1931). These dates show that the fashion persisted until long after less shallow conceptions had arisen. Possibly Biely's choral *Hunger March* (1933) and Szabo's tone-poem *Class War* (1933) should come under the same heading.

It was in 1922 or thereabouts that Soviet music really began to take shape. And from that time on, the standard of works inspired by patriotic and revolutionary subjects rose steadily. Although there was, naturally, a good deal of casting about during the reorganization period, most of the older composers adjusted themselves to the new conditions easily enough. Ippolitof-Ivanof (1859–1938), for instance, who had matured under national influences and always been attracted by the music of the Caucasus, played an important part, both as educator and as composer, in carrying out the Soviet policy of fostering the native music of the various races within the Union. Alexander Kastalsky (1856–1926), an authority on church- and folk-music, whose previous output had consisted mainly of liturgical music, apart from a few secular choral works (*Epic Tale*, *Glory*, and *Russia* among others) and one opera, *Clara Militch*, also fell into place quite naturally after the Revolution, and displayed great activity both as a composer and an organizer, his compositions including revolutionary hymns, arrangements of folk-songs with accompanying orchestras of native instruments, and *The Railway Train*, for chorus, piano, trumpet, and percussion. None of these has reached us yet.

The case of Reinhold Glière (*b.* 1875, at Kief) is especially noteworthy. His capacity for assimilation is shown by the fact that although of pure Belgian descent, as a composer he never displayed any non-Russian traits such as those that are so manifest in the music of the semi-Russian Cesar Cui, and here and there in Tchaikovsky's. His pre-Revolution output entitles him to an honourable place within the ranks of the more eclectic nationalists—somewhere between Glazunof and Gretchaninof, one might say, especially on the strength of works such as the tone-poems *Ilia Murometz* (his third symphony), *The Zaporogs*, *Trizna* (a funeral feast in old Russia).

Later, he applied this remarkable gift of his to the exploration of the possibilities of non-European music. His opera *Shakh Senem* (1934; commissioned by the Azerbaijan Republic) is entirely based on Turkish, Arabian, and Persian elements. In 1941 he started on another opera, *Leili and Medjun*, based on Uzbek elements. His other works include a ballet, *The Red Poppy*, another opera in Eastern style, *Gulsara*, and one entitled *1905*, particulars of which are not yet available.

But for a composer with a strong bent in one single direction such as Miaskovsky (*b.* 1881) the adjustment was bound to prove less easy. His pre-Revolution works show him very much under Tchaikovsky's influence, and, like him, lyrical, effusive, introspective, romantic, and pessimistic. Autobiographical notes in *Sovietskaya Muzyka* (June 1936) describe his efforts to alter his outlook and curb his impulses, revealing the qualms that accompanied the gestation of every major work of his:

Having reached the acme of pessimism with my sixth symphony, I succeeded in achieving a measure of objectivity in my seventh, and especially in my eighth. The tenth was an attempt, not very successful, at portraying the mental perturbation of Eugen, the hero of Pushkin's *The Bronze Horseman*. The eleventh was the expression of certain subjective moods. The twelfth did not come out quite as I had intended: it is in certain respects too abstractly formal, and I found neither the right form nor the right idiom for the finale. It embodies my intentions but superficially, and is not really convincing.

The thirteenth is thoroughly pessimistic in tone, and strange in character: the outcome of a blind impulse, and by now consigned to oblivion. The fourteenth is bright and dynamic enough; and although I do not feel the idiom to be, in vigour and freshness, all that could be desired, I regard the work as not deficient in vitality.

The fifteenth has been praised for its optimism and lyrical fervour. But it does not speak the language that I am still seeking, the language which I need in order to become really an artist of our time. Where is this to be found? I cannot tell, nor can I surmise what it will be. It is certainly futile to hope to discover it by exploring the old folk-songs of our countryside or the new popular songs of our cities, for one thing at least is clear: the musical idiom of socialist realism will have to be specifically instrumental, and so, very different from that of any vocal music in existence.

I do not regard my sixteenth (1935) as embodying a wholly successful solution of my problems either of form or of language, although it comes closer to the requirements of our time than any other work of mine.

Miaskovsky, who in the course of the winter 1942–1943 completed his twenty-fifth symphony, and whose output includes a good deal of other music, mainly instrumental, is regarded in Russia as one of the most representative Soviet composers, and held in high esteem. Elsewhere, his music has not attracted much attention; and the small proportion of it that has become known has been generally found discursive rather than imaginative, and not really adventurous. From the psychological point of view his is an extreme case of over-conscientiousness, no doubt. And this trait of character stands revealed even in his early works.

Among the composers who started after 1917, Yuri Shaporin (*b.* 1889) affords, by way of contrast, a perfect example of a thoroughly earnest and conscientious artist, with plenty of his own to say, whom the atmosphere around him has not in the least deflected from his natural course, or even unsettled. It may, it is true, have contributed to restrict his production. The fact that all his published works stand on a high level proves him to be endowed with an exacting self-critical sense, but there is plenty of evidence to show that he is a slow worker by nature. He began his professional education in 1913 only, and nothing of his appeared before the 'twenties.

Even his works on a small scale, the principal of which are two piano sonatas and two sets of songs, are few. His big works are a symphony (1932), a symphony cantata *On the Field of Kulikovo* (1937; the subject is the defeat of the Mongolian hordes that invaded Russia in 1360), and the opera *The Decembrists* (begun in 1925, finished in 1941). But he has also composed a quantity of incidental music to plays and of film-music, which, being unpublished, must be left out of count.

It is impossible not to feel that he remains ever true to his nature, not to perceive his thorough integrity of purpose and the firmness of his artistic outlook. His music, in which vernacular elements play a big part, maintains in most essentials the tradition of Russian nationalism at its best, is ripe, human, thoughtful, and poetic. The two song-sets (Tiutchef songs, 1926; and Pushkin songs, 1937) deserve to be widely known. In the symphony, he tried, he says, " to show the development of the fate of a human being in a great historical upheaval, the gradual transformation of individual consciousness in the progress of acceptance of the Revolution." [1] This special purpose (rather similar to that of Shostakovitch's fifth symphony, which will presently be referred to) does not in the least affect the quality of the music, except to a certain extent in the finale, entitled *March* (Campaign), which is in places, especially towards the end, rather coarse and crude. This symphony created as favourable an impression abroad as in Russia; and there is every reason to suppose that the same will happen with *On the Field of Kulikovo* and *The Decembrists*, of which glowing accounts have appeared.

Dimitri Shostakovitch (*b.* 1906) is in all technical respects as capable and well equipped as Shaporin, but otherwise the very antithesis of him. He started his career early, and made speedy headway. His music is not specifically national; what he owes to Russia's nineteenth-century innovators he acquired not directly

[1] Letter quoted, in translation, in Slonimsky's *Music since 1900* (London, 1937).

from them, but from the Western music upon which their influence first made itself felt.   His eclecticism now and then leads him astray. The first symphony (1925) that established his reputation throughout the world shows a maturity of invention and craftsmanship that would have been remarkable even in a far older composer.   It is, from end to end, alert, care-free, close-knit, live, genuinely imaginative music.   Of the works that followed, some are very good, but none comes near to the symphony in quality and scope.   They contained much that is derivative.   His second and third symphonies are, in parts, matter-of-fact and crude in a rather puerile way.

The opera *The Lady Macbeth of Mtsensk* shows him thoroughly adrift as regards both style and processes.   The score is a jumble of incompatible styles, recalling in turn the late Wagnerians, the Central European radicals, nineteenth-century grand opera and comic opera at their most conventional (he is a great believer in the efficacy of platitudes for parodic or even satirical purposes), and also—in the last act—Puccini.   Now and then, it is true, his imagination rises high; and certain scenes and orchestral episodes are most effective.   But on the whole, even though the official pronouncement that banned the music is open to discussion from the point of view of musical criticism pure and simple, there can be no doubt that here Shostakóvitch stands revealed at his worst.

Comparing *The Lady Macbeth* with the first symphony, one comes to the paradoxical conclusion that had it come first and the symphony later, the impression would have been that in the interval the composer had matured, overcome his defects, clarified and co-ordinated his style and methods, and developed a much-needed capacity for self-criticism.   As things are, one can but wonder what diverted him from the course he had started on with the symphony.

In the course of a debate on a later work of his, a piano quintet, Prokofief remarked:

> What astonishes me in this Piano Quintet is that so young a composer, at the height of his powers, should be so very much on his guard, and so carefully calculate every note.   He never takes a single risk.   One looks in vain for an impetus, a venture.

This may provide a clue.   Shostakovitch's best works before 1936 (first symphony; concerto for piano, trumpet, and strings; 'cello sonata) were those in which he concentrated (ingeniously, but certainly not adventurously) upon the possibilities of his medium and materials, without any ulterior purpose other than, let us grant, expression. He does not seem to be gifted with a strong sense of picturesque characterization, nor to be cut out for programme-music or dramatic music. So, maybe, it was when he yielded to fashions of the moment that he began to take risks by not remaining true to his own nature; and the crudities and other blemishes of *The Lady Macbeth* and certain previous works may have been the outcome of misguided calculations rather than of misguided impulses. The conclusion follows that his being compelled to take stock and make a fresh start might be all to the good. That it was to the good proved to be the general impression in Russia when, having made a fresh start after bowing to the inevitable, he came forth with his fifth symphony,[1] which bore the sub-title: "a Soviet artist's practical reply to just criticism", and in which he meant to depict "the re-education of a human mind through will-power and reason under the influence of the new ideals".

This was received with great enthusiasm in Russia: "a great achievement marking a new stage in the composer's evolution", the Moscow *Muzyka* proclaimed. Elsewhere it has met with a mixed reception. The critic of the Paris *Revue Musicale* found it "disappointing: a mere assemblage of commonplaces without one distinctive feature"—an opinion shared by the majority of London critics, including the present writer.

The sixth symphony, inspired by Mayakovsky's poem *Lenin*, was not unanimously praised, and has not been performed often outside Russia. The seventh, on the contrary, has attracted a good deal of attention in many countries, owing to the dramatic circumstances in which it came into being. The first movement was composed during the summer of 1941 in besieged Leningrad, and the remainder in Moscow and Kuibishef during the autumn. It is on a huge scale (it takes one hour and twenty-six minutes to play), and was conceived, the composer stated, as "a musical embodiment of the supreme ideal of patriotic war". Many of those who heard it regarded it as a splendid fulfilment of the composer's intentions; but others—including, once again, the present writer—found it long and monotonous most of the time, and not in the least convincing, nor out of the common even from the purely technical point of view. Of course it is not entirely devoid of interest; nor are, among his recent works, the previous two symphonies, a piano quintet, and a string quartet. But, comparing these works with the

---

[1] His fourth symphony (1936) he suppressed, being dissatisfied with it at rehearsals; and he also gave up his plans for an opera, whose subject was to be an episode of the civil war in the Urals, on which he had started working.

first symphony, one cannot help feeling that something has gone out of Shostakovitch which he has not yet succeeded in recapturing.

To understand the reproof of formalism which Shostakovitch and others have incurred, it is essential to realize that Soviet critics use the term to connote not, as is usual, addiction to stereotyped devices mechanically applied for purposes of working-out (or, rather, filling-in), but the inclination to concentrate on problems of texture and structure, however novel and pregnant these may be. It was levelled at Gabriel Popof (*b.* 1904), whose chamber-music, composed in the early 'twenties, had won praise, and whose symphony had been awarded, jointly with Shaporin's, the Union of Composers' prize in 1932. According to an article in *Sovietskaya Muzyka* (June 1934) this symphony testified to "a genuine sense of, and an active participation in, the life of the period". Later, opinion veered. L. Grinberg (*ib.*, March 1936) declared that "the prize had been awarded on the strength of the piano version. The orchestral performance caused the verdict to be reversed."

The few works by Popof that reached this country proved to be of a radical, experimental order, and showed affinities with Hindemith's and Alban Berg's. Heinrich Litinsky (*b.* 1901), who shows similar affinities, but is more classically inclined, is a fine technician, whose output consists entirely of instrumental music—(string quartets, sonatas for violin solo, viola solo, 'cello solo, two symphonies, piano concerto). He was even more vehemently impugned on the count of formalism. His fifth quartet, based not on abstract elements of his own devising, but on Turkmenian tunes, was hailed by Ostretsof (in *Sovietskaya Muzyka*, March 1934) as marking a welcome change in his outlook.

> Issue is joined between the old individual consciousness and the new, that of the fighter and builder of the socialist community. May Litinsky devote his great talent to carrying out the duties that lie before him and all Soviet artists.

Later, however, the question of his formalistic tendencies and of the character they gave to his teaching cropped up again (*ib.*, March 1936). Of late years, no tidings of new compositions by him or by Popof have come through.

Another composer who has been criticized for his formalistic tendencies is Leonid Polovinkin (*b.* 1894; he made his début in 1924 only). Like the composers so far mentioned here from Shaporin onwards, he is keenly interested in the possibilities of his medium, apart from any question of ulterior purpose. No doubt certain of his works are abstract and complex: for instance, the set *Telescopes* for full-sized symphony orchestra, and the *Magnets* for piano. But he certainly regards music as a means of communicating with his audiences, and not as mere mental gymnastics.

Obviously he has devoted much thinking to the ways and means most likely to suit his every purpose. Among his early works are five piano sonatas in more or less traditional form. To the fifth he gave the sub-title " last sonata ", which was regarded, quite rightly, as an affirmation of his resolve to break fresh ground in the province of form. It also includes five symphonies, the third being entitled " Romantic: the October Revolution ", and the fourth dedicated to the Red Army. In his piano pieces *Happenings*, he set out " to evoke, not events in the outer world, but happenings within his own soul ". The incidental music to the play *The Hero* (a Russian translation of Synge's *Playboy of the Western World*) revealed, it is said, a rare sense of comedy and satire.

But most significant of all is the fact that he is the musical director of the Moscow Theatre for Children, and in that capacity, as well as in his capacity as a composer, has done excellent work there. A full-size opera, *The Fisherman and the Fish* (1936), was one of his many contributions to its repertory. According to Poliakof (*Sovietskaya Muzyka*, February 1937):

> The subject was derived from a Pushkin tale, the composer writing his own libretto. It is, like those of Rimsky-Korsakof's *Tsar Saltan* and *Golden Cockerel*, fantastic, humorous, and satirical, but dealt with straightforwardly, not taken as a pretext for a display of virtuosity in treatment. Polovinkin's music is simple and expressive, does not contain actual folk-tunes, but is vernacular in accent and colour, bright, and racy, showing here and there—and especially in the underseas scenes—the influence of Rimsky-Korsakof. At certain spots, there is, perhaps, too much stylizing, and certain grotesque effects are too deliberate. But as a whole, the opera is of great artistic value.

One critic, it is true (L. Grinberg, already mentioned in connection with Popof), found the work insincere, cold, soulless, thoroughly out of keeping with the teachings of the *Pravda* article on abstraction and falsity in music: but this view seems to have found little or no endorsement. Another interesting work is the " heroic " symphony for children, *Keepers of the Frontier*. Many of his songs and piano pieces are designed for children.

The examples accessible here testify to his skill, imagination, and sense of fitness and proportion.   They are far too few to convey an adequate impression of his musical personality, but they certainly make one long to explore his output further.

Considerations of spirit and feeling being given precedence over considerations of invention and technique, it happens that works found satisfactory from the former point of view are praised more highly than others that rise to a far higher musical level. Thus, Ivan Dzerjinsky's opera *Quiet Flows the Don* (1935) met with an enthusiastic reception, though the composer (*b*. 1909), mainly self-taught, revealed his lack of experience, and even of ambition so far as craftsmanship was concerned, all too clearly:

> It is deeply to be regretted that in so luminous and fresh a work, the effort to achieve realistic truth should have borne but little fruit. Dzerjinsky lacks the required ability. The orchestra plays an insignificant part, and variety is altogether lacking. Still, *Quiet Flows the Don* is one of the most significant Soviet operas.
>
> (Budiakovsky in *Sovietskaya Muzyka*, November 1935.)

His second opera, *Virgin Soil Upturned* (1937), won unqualified approval:

> He has thoroughly overcome his tendency to rest satisfied with improvisation. The simplicity and sincerity of the musical language, the high political bearing of the subject (life in a Soviet village in the period of collectivism) and the realism of the treatment embody ideals towards which all Soviet artists should strive.
>
> (The same writer, *ib.*, October 1937.)

Among the other composers whose natural inclination to write music easily accessible to the masses has won high praise are Marian Koval (*b*. 1907), Alexander Davidenko (1899–1934), Alexei Zhivotof (*b*. 1904), Irakli (or Vano) Muradeli (*b*. 1908), and Dimitri Zhelobinsky (*b*. 1913). A name that stands out is that of Aram Khatchaturian (*b*. 1904), whom Soviet Russia regards as one of her most truly and fully representative composers. He made his début with a trio for clarinet, violin, and piano, a Dance Suite for orchestra, and a violin sonata, all three based on folk-tunes from his native Armenia, and testifying to a strong national feeling and to an inborn sense of melody, colour, and instrumental treatment.   A symphony followed (1934).   To how great an extent it fulfilled the expectations aroused by his previous achievements is shown by Khubof's declar-ing (*Sovietskaya Muzyka*, Sept. 1939): "It occupies in our symphonic music as important a place as *Quiet Flows the Don* in our dramatic music."   His methods, as often as not, are rhapsodic rather than architectural; and he does not always steer clear of diffusiveness and redundance.   Both his defects and his qualities are manifest in his two concertos (for piano and violin respectively), which are dramatic, romantic in tone, with a good deal of vivid, at times intense, colour; and there can be no doubt that every new work of his marked a step forwards.   The strong attraction exercised on him by the traditional music of his country enabled him to fall into place quite naturally in the ranks of the national Armenian school which had begun to take shape under the leadership of Komitas Kervorkian (1869–1925) and N. Tigranian (1856–1936) long before the days when the Soviets started fostering the development of national schools in all the newly liberated and organized republics of the Union.   But, all told, nineteenth-century Russian music contributed as much to his artistic formation as Armenian folk-music did.   His musical style and methods owe far more to those of the Russian nationalists than is the case with the wholly and exclusively Armenian composers of yesterday and to-day.   The forms he resorts to are clasiscal forms of European tradition: that is, forms acclimatized in Russia, but not in Armenia.   The melodic elements he uses are, for the most part, wholly Armenian, whether they are actual folk-tunes or not; and Russian experts have noted that many of his harmonies reflect the tone quality and harmonic properties of Armenian instruments.

In his *Ode to Stalin*, for orchestra with final chorus (1937), he uses jointly tunes of songs on Stalin composed in Armenia, Georgia, and Azerbaijan, successfully solving, we are told, the arduous problem of combining these dissimilar elements in a smooth and consistent symphonic texture.   His more recent ballet, *Happi-ness*, based on Armenian folk-tunes, is said to.be one of his most felicitous works, and should be well worth a trial here as soon as the score is accessible.

Comparatively better known to us are Anatol Alexandrof (*b.* 1888), Dimitri Kabalevsky (*b.* 1904), Vissarion Shebalin (*b.* 1902), and Samuel Feinberg (*b.* 1890).   Judging by the portions of their output that have reached us, they are able, eclectic, and cultured rather than enterprising.   Kabalevsky has composed four symphonies, the third of which is in the form of a *Requiem* with chorus in memory of Lenin, and an opera, *The Master of Clamecy*, after Romain Rolland's novel *Colas Brugnon*; Shebalin, chamber-music and orchestral music, including four symphonies, the third on a vast scale and choral, the text being taken from Mayakovsky's poem *Lenin*. Alexandrof is very conservative, and chiefly interested in the smaller forms of music; but he has written two symphonic suites and two operas.

Feinberg holds an honourable place among the minor poets of the Soviet school. His output consists mainly of piano music (suites, eight sonatas, and pieces based on folk-tunes from various republics of the Union) and songs, including fine settings of poems by Pushkin, composed in 1937. A few months later, it was announced by the Russian critic Leonid Sabaneief that he had renounced com-position, being discouraged by the public's lack of response. In actual fact, he came forth in 1938 with a set of twenty-five Chuvash songs, provided by him with elaborate and effective, but not always suitable, piano accompaniments.[1]

Among the many composers whose music remains either alto-gether or almost unknown outside Russia are, to begin with (apart from the leaders of the nationalist Jewish movement, who will be referred to in the next chapter), Knipper, Liatoshinsky, Pash-chenko, and Shekhter.

Lev Knipper (*b.* 1898) is a well-equipped composer with a strong intellectual bent, interested in problems of form, harmony, and orchestration. He has composed seven symphonies, and many other orchestral works, including *Miniatures* for children and music based on folk-tunes from Tadjikistan—notably the Suite *Vantch*, which Professor Belaief regards as an important landmark, and which will be referred to in Chapter XVI, jointly with Shekhter's *Turkmenia* mentioned in the next paragraph. His first important work, *The Legend of the Plaster Buddha* for orchestra (1924), reveals a marked capacity for grotesque effects, which is also mani-fest in his ballet *Satanella*. His third symphony, in which he uses Siberian folk-tunes, is inscribed to the Far East Red Army; his fifth, to the working and fighting Soviet youth; and his sixth, to the Red Cavalry. This came in for sharp criticism, and was described as dry, abstract, formalistic, and empty. The seventh, inspired by the subject *The Defence of the Soviet Land*, has a circumstantial programme. Signs of an inclination to follow Tchaikovsky's effusive methods (already noticed in certain earlier works by a few

[1] Sabaneief is often unreliable on facts and dates: but on this occasion, he may have got hold of a rumour, or a sally uttered by Feinberg in a moment of ill-temper.

critics, Gerald Abraham among others) are said to be manifest in it.
Boris Liatoshinský (*b.* 1893), said to be a bold and brilliant harmonist
and orchestrator, has composed two operas, *The Golden Hoop* and
Shchors (evoking a famous hero of the Ukraine). Andrei Pash-
chenko (*b.* 1883) is described as an eclectic, but one who shows
marked affinities with the nineteenth-century nationalists. Although he is one of the many Soviet composers who started on their
career late (he began his professional education in 1914 only), he
has an important list of works to his credit, notably four operas;
an oratorio, *Lenin*; seven symphonies; instrumental works of
various kinds, and choral music in great variety.

Boris Shekhter (*b.* 1900), after composing a number of instrumental works which attracted no particular notice, made a special
study of Turkmenian music, and scored a great success with his
suite *Turkmenia*. His other principal works are a Symphonic
Dithyramb composed for the twentieth anniversary of the Russian
Revolution (1937), and a piano concerto (1938).

Other unknown quantities are Golubef, said to be remarkably
gifted; Vladimir Shcherbatchef (not to be confused with Nikolai
Shcherbatchef, a minor member of the Balakiref group); Boris
Asafief (*b.* 1884), who acquired a great reputation through his
critical writings, signed "Igor Gliebof", and who, during the
'thirties, turned out a number of operas and ballets; Boris Mokro-
ussof (*b.* 1909; his principal compositions are symphonic works,
including an *Anti-Fascist Symphony* and an opera, *Tchapaief*, the
characters in which include Lenin and Stalin); Starokadomsky;
Yurovsky; and Kortchmaref. Evgheny Golubef (*b.* 1910) among
other things has composed piano sonatas, a string quartet, a
symphony, and an oratorio, *The Return of the Sun*; Tikhon Khren-
nikof (*b.* 1913), a piano concerto, a symphony, and an opera, *In the
Storm*; Shcherbatchef (*b.* 1889), four symphonies and an opera,
Anna Kolossova; Mikhail Starokadomsky (*b.* 1901), an opera, an
oratorio, a symphony, a violin concerto, two orchestral suites, and
other instrumental works, including (a great rarity in Russia) an
organ concerto; Vladimir Yurovsky (*b.* 1913), a symphony, a
symphonic suite, *Moscow Carnival*, a violin concerto, and an opera,
Concerning Opanas (an episode of the civil war in the Ukraine);
Klementi Kortchmaref (*b.* 1899), operas, a ballet (said to be eclectic
in style) and a choral symphony, *Holland*, the text consisting of
translated Dutch revolutionary poems. Nikolai Budashkin (*b.*
1910) is a pupil of Miaskovsky, very much under the influence of
his teacher and of Tchaikovsky.

A few women composers—the first to appear in Russia—must

now be mentioned.[1]   The eldest of these, Julia Weisberg (b. 1879), had all but completed her curriculum at the Petersburg Conservatoire when she was expelled, in 1905, for joining in demonstrations against autocratic and reactionary officialdom.   During the following years she turned out a number of compositions, chiefly orchestral.   But it was only after the Revolution that she came to the fore (when she devoted herself almost exclusively to vocal and dramatic music).   She has a genuine gift for lyrical expression; and also for comedy, as shown in her racy, lively opera *Gulsara*— in which, as in many other works of hers, Eastern elements play a big part.   She has composed a good deal of music for children, including operas.

Barbara Gaigerova (b. 1903) also deserves attention.   Her output includes four symphonies, two string quartets, a symphonic suite on Caucasian themes, and other instrumental music based on Asiatic elements, songs, and piano music.   Only a few songs have reached us so far.   Three other names occur: Nina Biriukova, Zara Levina, and Nina Makarova.   No particulars about them or works of theirs are available.

This enormous list is far from exhaustive.   There may have been unintentional omissions.   A number of obviously non-representative, mediocre, or immature composers were intentionally left out; and also a few who attracted attention but for a fleeting moment: for instance, Nikolai Roslavetz (b. 1881), whose only assets seem to be a remorseless rationalism nurtured on modern innovations from Debussy's to Schönberg's; Alexander Mossolof (b. 1900), whose output during the 'twenties was considerable and varied, but of whom only one work, the ultra-realistic tone picture *Steel Foundry*, seems to have been considered worthy of notice[2]; and Alexander Waulin, concerning whom no information is available except a couple of articles by Igor Gliebof praising (in 1919 or thereabouts) his chamber-music and giving excellent reasons for so doing. Many others, who glowed awhile in the firmament of Soviet music in the light of premature praise, have vanished in darkness after a brief, and not in the least meteoric, career.

On the whole, the list given here is likely to be, if anything, overcomprehensive.   And after making all due allowances, one cannot

---

[1] Only three European countries have women composers to show; the other two are England and France.

[2] He was dismissed in 1936, for disciplinary reasons, from the Union of Soviet Composers, which put a stop to his productivity until 1939, when he was reinstated.   The only work of his mentioned since then is a concerto for harp and orchestra.

help wondering how much of all that music is likely to endure in Russia and to be found acceptable elsewhere, ideology or no ideology. The question becomes even more puzzling when the many national and regional schools that remain to be mentioned are taken into account.

CHAPTER XVI

OTHER NATIONAL SCHOOLS OF THE UNION

To include these national schools in a survey of Soviet musical activities is natural, and indeed unavoidable: but for the Soviets' policy of fostering, by all possible means, their birth and growth, very few of them (and especially of those that are not Russian, or not even Slavonic, but purely Asiatic) would have come into being. And those that do come into being do so under conditions very similar to those that obtain within the musical orbit of Soviet Russia.

It is part of the Soviet Government's general policy to encourage every nation within the Union to practise music and composition. Composers are invited to contrive, out of the elements of the native music of each race, an idiom and style suitable for use in symphonic art, but free—so far as possible—from Western conventions; and also new structural principles based either on native usage or on the inherent properties of these elements, in the same way as the forms of Western music are based on the properties of the major–minor system.

This is done, on the one hand, by sending Russian composers to study vernacular music on the spot, assimilate it, and use it, and on the other hand by providing educational facilities and various kinds of encouragement for native composers, and also ensuring performance and publication of their works.

There are national schools, more or less flourishing or merely budding, not only in the European or near-European republics of Ukraine, White Russia, Georgia, and Armenia, but also in many of the Asiatic. Some of these schools had begun to take shape under the old *régime*: the Ukrainian with Lissenko, the Armenian, and also the national Jewish school of which Alexander Krein and Gniessin were the original leaders. A start had been made in Azerbaijan too, by Uzeir Hadjibekof, who in 1908 came forth with a play, *Leily and Medjun*, the incidental music of which consisted of native tunes used without much elaboration.

The music of many of the above peoples, and especially the Ukrainian, Georgian, Armenian, and Jewish, contains little or nothing that is incompatible with European practice and usage. Elements from all four had, in fact, already found place in nineteenth-century music, Western or Russian; and no complex technical problems arise in relation to their use. But elsewhere, difficulties of all kinds crop up.

Turkmenian and Uzbek music may well serve to illustrate the point. Both have aroused great interest among Russian composers and scholars. Professors Belaief and Uspensky; the joint authors of a big book on the subject, inform us that Turkmenian music is a highly organized art, the product of a culture of long standing. It has its distinctive scales, melodies, rhythms, and forms, most of them dissimilar to those of European music. Likewise, according to the same authorities, Uzbekistan has a musical culture of its own, rooted in a very old tradition. Its native tunes do not lend themselves to treatment on European lines; and the treatment they receive at the hands of native composers does not seem capable of extension to suit present-day requirements. " It is most difficult ", Martynof remarked (*Sovietskaya Muzyka*, Jan. 1938) with reference to Uspensky and Glière's treatment of Uzbek tunes in the scores of *Farkhad and Shirin* and *Giulsara*, " to find suitable harmonizations for these tunes. The native scales are in many respects peculiar. It is necessary to discover the boundless possibilities latent in the native monody; and this the arrangers have not always succeeded in doing, although here and there, especially in *Giulsara*, there are instances of effective polyphonic choral writing. But, generally speaking, the primitive, strictly ethnographic forms so far in use do not suffice: the experience of world-wide operatic culture must contribute to the enrichment of the new national forms and styles."

Likewise Stepanof (*ib.*, Feb. 1940): " The European technique applied in *Farkhad* and *Giulsara* is not altogether adequate. The character of the melos is at times veiled, and thrown out of balance." According to the same writer, Vassilenko and the Uzbek composer Ashrafi, in the score of the opera *Buran*, come far nearer a satisfactory solution. It is also said that in his latest opera, *Ker Oglu* (the Blind Man's Son), Hadjibekof did not quite succeed in discovering the right way to deal with the native tunes of Azerbaijan; but that Glière, in his *Shakh Senem*, comes far nearer the mark.

There are many instances of similar collaboration. *Farkhad and Shirin*, originally a play with a small amount of incidental music, like *Leily and Medjun*, was remodelled by Uspensky with the help of two other composers, Zweifel and Mushel. For *Giulsara*, Glière used tunes selected for the purpose by three native specialists. He also provided, with the help of Sadykof, more elaborate music for *Leily and Medjun*. Hadjibekof and Khatchaturian were sent to help the younger Turkmenian composers to find their feet; Vlassof and Féré to faraway Kirghizia. There they composed, in 1936, *Altyn Kyz*, a musical play that was described as a very promising first attempt to exploit the Kirghiz vernacular; and immediately afterwards, with the collaboration of the Kirghiz composer Abdylas Maldybaef, the opera *Adjal Orduna* (Life) evoking the revolt of the Kirghiz against the tsarist régime.

The perspectives opened by Turkmenian music have attracted several Russians, notably Mossolof, Vassilenko, and Shekhter. Russian critics agree in regarding Mossolof's *Turkmenian Nights* and Vassilenko's *Turkmenian Suite* as far less significant than Shekhter's orchestral suite *Turkmenia*. The fact that the score is available here, and that performances of it have taken place, makes it possible to consider more closely the question of European composers and listeners in relation to Turkmenian music.

Uspensky and Belaief stress the fact that Turkmenian native music is rich in subtle forms of variation and working-out. They also inform us that it aims at psychological expression rather than at mere external effectiveness. Shekhter, in composing his Suite, was not in the least concerned with European practice and standards. The work is uncompromisingly Turkmenian in idiom, style, and form. Many features of the new region he invites us to explore will probably baffle us or escape our notice.

This is only natural, after all. The widespread platitude that music is a universal language does not stand examination. The truth is that, as Nietzsche puts it, "the language of music is neither universal nor independent of time conditions. It is one whose inner laws depend upon the culture of one region or period." Unless they comprehend and (what is even more important) feel the inner laws of Turkmenian music, composers will do no more than manipulate its elements more or less arbitrarily and mechanically. And one cannot help fearing lest listeners, by the same token, miss not only the psychological significance of native Turkmenian music, but also that wealth and versatility of development which experts have praised so highly. Rhythms and colour-schemes may prove easier to perceive than the underlying melodic continuity, diversity, and logic. The exotic rather than the human elements will stand out. It is only fair to add that an achievement such as Shekhter's *Turkmenia* goes a long way towards dispelling all such fears: it is as convincing as it is brilliant of its kind.

The movement, of course, is still in its early, experimental, at times merely tentative stages. Yet activity reigns from one end of the Union to the other, composition or preliminary research and

study being carried out among the Yamals of the Samoyed penin-
sula, the Tadjiks of the Pamir, the Buriat-Mongols of the Baikal,
the Oyrots of the Altai, the Yakuts of Eastern Siberia, the Tartars,
Kalmuks, Kirghiz, Mordvinians, and others.   And while Russian
composers are striving to build up a vernacular repertory for the
people of the new Republics, the composers cropping up in those
Republics are repaying them in kind by tackling Russian subjects.
The opera *Katchkyn* (the Fugitive, an episode of the Pugachef
uprising), by the Tatar composer Nazyb Djyganof, is not only the
first Tatar opera, but also the first opera on a national Russian
subject composed by a non-Russian on the basis of the vernacular
music of his own country.

Naturally, it would be foolish to expect startling revelations to
follow as a matter of course.   But at least those peoples, in proportion as culture spreads among them, will learn to appreciate the
higher, more elaborate forms of musical art, as evolved in Europe,
and be helped in acquiring the needful experience by the existence
of a repertory of examples in which, as Glinka in his time had put
it, they will feel quite at home—which is, after all, what matters
most.   And maybe a number of the new national works will win a
place in the world-repertory.   No experiment of the kind has
ever been attempted before on anything like so comprehensive a
scale.

So far, it is by the composers of the older schools, and those that
have longest been in contact with European tradition, that the best
results have been obtained: *e.g.*, the Armenian and the Ukrainian.
The Armenian school is the oldest.   Its first leaders were Christopher
Kara-Murza (1854–1902), Makar Ekmalian (1855–1909), and
Nikolai Tigranian (1856–1936).   The first-named published many
arrangements of folk-songs.   Ekmalian composed church music
and songs.   Tigranian assiduously studied and collected Armenian,
Iranian, Turkish, and Kurdish music, and published a large number
of piano arrangements of songs and dance tunes.   Komitas Kervorkian (1869–1935) not only did much to encourage the study of
national Armenian music by his teachings and his remarkably fine
editions of choral and other examples, but composed a number of
original works, very few of which were published.   The manuscripts
of most of them were destroyed by him in the course of a cruel
mental illness that incapacitated him for work from 1916 onwards.

Spiridion Melikian (1880–1933), a pupil of his, also did excellent
work on similar lines.   His principal original composition is
Akhtamar, a setting for chorus and orchestra of a poem by Ovas
Tumanian.   Romanos Melikian (1882–1935), whose output, not

large, consists chiefly of songs and a few instrumental works, also played a big part in organizing the musical life of the country. Alexander Spendiarof (1871–1928), a pupil of Rimsky-Korsakof, did not evince any special interest in native Armenian music until after the Revolution, and but for his later work would be remembered only as one of the minor Russian nationalists. In 1924 he settled in Erivan, and the works he composed there—notably the opera *Almast* and orchestral *Erivan Études*—were important contributions to the formation of a national Armenian style. Armen Tigranian (*b.* 1871, a pupil of Ekmalian) composed his opera *Anush*, on an Armenian subject, in 1912. He remodelled it in 1932, and it was produced in 1935. His output includes incidental music to plays, one of the *Leily and Medjun*, a popular Eastern subject already mentioned in connection with other composers.

Among the younger Armenians, apart from Khatchaturian already mentioned, the principal are Grigory Egiazarof (*b.* 1908), who, like Spendiarof, was influenced at first by the Russian national school, and also made a special study of Tatar music, but whose compositions (songs, piano music, ballet *A Drop of Mead*) are unmistakably Armenian in style; and Aro Stepanian, who has to his credit, among other things, three operas, songs, and a Suite for 'cello and piano. Others, among whom are S. Barkhudarian, N. Martytchian, V. Umr-Shatom, and D. Shvedof—are working in Georgia.

The history of the Ukrainian school begins with the activities of Nikolai Lissenko (1842–1912), who studied the native folk-music, published most valuable sets of it, and composed most industriously, mainly piano music, and also operas—ten in number, the most interesting being *Taras Bulba, Sappho,* and the *Æneid*. It is said that the last-named two, despite their non-national subjects, marked an interesting stage in the formation of a national Ukrainian style. Lissenko, we are told, was gifted with a particularly keen and subtle sense of intonation, and his recitatives are exemplary.

Taras Bulba was not produced during his lifetime. When the question of producing it on the occasion of the twentieth anniversary of the liberation of Ukraine (1937) arose, it was discovered that part of the original orchestral score was lost, and that part of what remained stood in need of remodelling and expansion. Revutsky (see below) took charge of the remodelling, Liatoshinsky of the re-orchestration. In this new form, the work was successfully produced.

The foundation of the Kharkof opera house in 1924 proved a great stimulus. At the 1935 Moscow Conference on Soviet Opera, it was stated that between 1924 and 1934, twelve Ukrainian composers had between them added sixteen operas to the national repertory. The most distinguished members of the school are Lev Revutsky (*b.* 1889) and Boris Liatoshinsky (*b.* 1895). The former is regarded as the leader, after Lissenko, of the national movement. His output is small; it includes songs, piano pieces, arrangements of folk-songs, and two symphonies (the second took a first prize at an all-Ukrainian competition in 1927). Liatoshinsky's principal works are the operas *The Golden Hoop* and *Shchors*, an Overture on four Ukrainian themes (also awarded a first prize in 1927), two symphonies, and chamber-music. He commands a brilliant, versatile technique and a highly developed sense of harmony and of orchestral colour. Feodor Akimenko will be mentioned in the next chapter.

Very little information as to the musical output of Georgia has come forth so far—as often as not nothing but names of composers and titles of works, with maybe a few brief general remarks. The pioneer was Zakharia Paliashvili (1872–1933), whose principal compositions are songs, choral works, and three operas, the first produced in 1913. He has done much fine work on native Georgian music, studying, notably, the idiosyncrasies of its peculiar, highly developed polyphony, which he extended considerably in pursuance of his own purposes. Mentions occur in *Sovietskaya Muzyka* of good choral music by Arakishvili, Tsagareishvili, Kokeladze, symphonic music by Mshvelidze, Kiladze, Kereselidze, piano concertos by Balanchivadze and Avetisof. Most of the above named, and also Tusky, Gokielsky, and Andriashvili, have composed operas. Two women composers are also named: Olga Baramishvili and D. Slianova. One has the impression that the repertory of Georgian music is particularly worth exploring, and its growth worth following.

In White Russia, a national school is said to be taking shape. Operas by Shcheglof, Bogatyref, Tykotsky, and Turenkof were produced in 1939. A ballet by Kroshner and works by Liuban and Polonsky containing more or less vernacular elements are mentioned. A fairly long list of White Russian composers, without any particulars, was given in the September 1939 issue of *Sovietskaya Muzyka*.

The national Jewish movement began a few years before 1914. Its leaders, Alexander Krein and Mikhail Gniessin (both born in 1883), did not incline to nationalism until comparatively far advanced in their career; and even afterwards they did not invariably follow a nationalist line, but often composed works in which Jewish elements played no part whatever (so did, by the way, Ernest Bloch, also one of the foremost exponents of Jewish nationalism). Krein's early works are eclectic in style. He developed an interest in Jewish traditional music at the age of twenty-five; the firstfruits of his studies were two sets of *Hebraic Sketches* for clarinet and string quartet (1909–1910), *Songs of the Ghetto*, a *Hebraic Caprice* for violin and piano, a cantata, *Kaddish*, for tenor, chorus, and orchestra, the opera *Zagmuth*, and the tone-poem *Birobidjan* followed. In between came important works of a non-Hebraic order: the trilogy *The Soviet Shock Brigade* for orchestra and chorus (texts from the writings of Marx, Lenin, and Stalin), a Threnody in memory of Lenin, and a ballet, *Laurencia*, the subject of which is taken from Lope de Vega's play *Fuente Ovejuna*. The various essays on him that have appeared in Russia say that his music reveals a highly strung, deeply emotional nature.

The same is said of Gniessin, whose artistic evolution followed a similar course. His early works are eclectic in style, romantic in tone, not in any way nationalist. The principal are the tone-poems *After Shelley*, *The Conqueror Worm* (after Poe), a dithyramb for voices and orchestra in memory of the painter Vroubel, and a Requiem (for piano quintet) in memory of Rimsky-Korsakof.

Another group of works consists of dramatic music in which he uses a declamation of his own devising, the text being taken from old Greek tragedies and Jewish plays. And the Jewish works include, among others, variations for string quartet on a Jewish theme, *Songs of the Old Country* for orchestra, and the operas *Abraham's Youth* and *The Maccabeans*. The latest work of his of which mention has reached us is a *Symphonic Monument* for chorus and orchestra, commemorating the revolutions of 1905 and 1917.

Grigory Krein (*b.* 1880), Alexander's brother, also played a part in the nationalist movement, but seems to have done little in composition until he reached the age of forty. His output consists chiefly of chamber-music, most of it unpublished; it includes a violin concerto, two piano concertos, and *Lenin*, a set of three symphonic episodes. All these works have come in for high praise.

Alexander Veprik (*b.* 1899) is a thoughtful and versatile composer, endowed with a fine sense of expression, and, like Grigory Krein, fond of experimenting in complex, dissonant harmonies. Of his specifically Hebraic works, the most characteristic is *Songs and Dances of the Ghetto* for orchestra. The list of his works included *1905*, a set of five episodes for orchestra and chorus; *Song of Joy* and *Song of Mourning* for orchestra; a tone-picture, *Stalinstan*; and miscellaneous symphonic works.

All the information we have conveys the impression that the music of the above four reaches a high technical level, that most of it is romantic, charged with emotion, but not unrestrainedly so, and seldom over-effusive; and that it should be well worth knowing.

CHAPTER XVII

RUSSIAN COMPOSERS IN OTHER COUNTRIES

THE emigration of Russian composers after 1917 scattered them far and wide. The consequences cannot be usefully studied before it becomes possible to view things from the right distance. It is a question of the influence of racial and hereditary impulses and habits *versus* that of education and surroundings. To tackle it without full knowledge of each composer's genealogy and of the circumstances of each particular case would be futile; but one cannot ignore it even in the most summary of surveys.

Much depends, of course, upon each composer's nature, and his capacity for adjusting such knowledge and power as he may acquire to suit his own purpose. He may be more or less amenable to influences, musical and other. The surroundings, too, may be a misfit. One may surmise that Stravinsky, had he never left Russia, would have followed exactly the same course: but one cannot help wondering how Mussorgsky would have conceived and solved his problems had he lived in Germany. It will be obvious that there is no possibility of including these various orders of considerations in the present brief chapter, in which no attempt at classification except according to the country in which the composers settled will be attempted.

A number of them are in France; notably among the older men, Nikolai Tcherepnin (see p. 79) and also Thomas Hartmann (*b.* 1886), educated partly in Moscow, partly in Munich, a versatile, eclectic composer with a strong bent towards nationalism, whose principal works are a *Symphonic Poem*, a violin, a piano, and a 'cello concerto, an opera, *Flionushka*, and a ballet, *Beauty and the Beast.*

Nikolai Obukhof (*b.* 1892, educated at St. Petersburg) went to Paris in 1918, and received lessons from Ravel and Marcel Orban. The most disconcerting of Russian composers, he may have been influenced, at the start, by Scriabin's outlook: but not so by his musical methods. As deliberately as Scriabin, he strives to use music for special ulterior purposes; but spiritually, he is the very antipode of that worldly and deliberate calculator. There is nothing sophisticated about him. Nothing in his works is conceived or carried out in view of its possible effect on the audience's emotions or nerves.   On the contrary, his music is a perfect example of what has been termed expressionism—that is, according to the one and only clear definition even given of the term, " the endeavour to express, not the external world, but the inner self of the artist, the ego engrossing the interest so much that the external object either disappears or becomes unrecognizable, all external reality being suppressed ".

In his morbid, savage striving towards achieving the desired expression, he draws upon all manner of sounds obtainable from instruments and voices: sequences of chords every one of which consists of all twelve notes of the tempered scale, gasps and shrieks in the vocal parts, and notes far outside the compass of the human voice, as well as glissandi now through a semitone, now through an octave and more.   On paper, it seems uncouth and meaningless. According to notices from competent judges, it is quite effective. Roland-Manuel, a French critic who is, if anything, over-fastidious in such matters, wrote in the *Revue Musicale*:

> The sonority is skilfully balanced, the result being a crystal-like, icy perspicuity.   It carries us into an unknown, terrifying world, peopled with dread phantoms.   It often is torture to the ear, but the remorseless tormentor he is shows impressive sensitiveness and lucid musical skill.

Ravel, too, considered the music " instinct with pathetic force, and unmistakably betokening genius ".   Boris de Schloezer wrote (*Revue Musicale*, July 1926) that his scoring was first-rate.   " I dislike the very principle of his music," he added, " but its originality and power, the sincerity and earnestness of the thinking, command respect even from adversaries."

Other points made by commentators are: the music is static, practically motionless.   It is also shapeless, but holds together owing to its psychological unity.   It was introduced to Paris audiences as early as 1921, but since then has made little headway, despite the performances that took place at intervals.   It consists chiefly of settings of liturgical or mystical texts, the principal work being *The Book of Life*, an enormous oratorio of which only parts are composed so far.   Very few works are published.   Provisionally, one feels that the verdict which d'Indy passed at the time when Debussy's *Pelléas et Mélisande* was bewildering the Paris musical circles: " not music in the usual sense of the word, but something altogether different and novel, to be understood and judged for what it is ", could be aptly applied to the published examples.

Igor Markevitch (*b.* 1912) left Russia at an early age, and was educated in Paris. He displayed, while still in his teens, a precocity no less striking than that of Shostakovitch, a sinfonietta (1928), a piano concerto, a concerto grosso (1929), a choral cantata (1930), and a ballet, *Rebus* (1931), in turn attracting favourable notice, and he has progressed consistently ever since. In his early works, the influence of Stravinsky is noticeable. Later, he showed certain spiritual affinities with Obukhof: " There is a mystical side to his nature. He seeks to impart to his music a deep humanitarian feeling. His art should, he thinks, bear its part in the reshaping of the social order, and enable us to penetrate more deeply into the world of the spirit " (P. Le Flem in Grove's *Dictionary*).

But there the resemblance ends: he is versatile, self-possessed, skilful at planning, marshalling, and constructing. His musical style is more or less in line with modern usage, although his methods are in some respects peculiar enough to have given rise to comments of an unwonted and unexpected kind. For instance, one critic, P. Souvtchinsky (*Revue Musicale*, July 1932), suggested that his aural sense was abnormal—" astigmatic " metaphorically speaking. This anomaly, he averred, led him to overlook the unstable nature of discords: " whence, in his work, long stretches of slow-moving, yet flowing, substantial, and significant music, behaving in a way quite its own. As Cézanne's astigmatism led him to find new proportions and relations in his object-models, so is Markevitch able to discover new proportions and realities in the world of sound." The Belgian critic A. de Graef described the score of his ballet *The Flight of Icarus* (1933) as " disconcerting, but moving and powerful; so definite, straightforward, and perspicuous in its merciless logic that it seems, at times, unreal and hostile " (*Revue Musicale*, June 1935). After the Paris performance of his oratorio *Paradise Lost* (1935), L. Kochnitsky struck a curious note: " Markevitch composed this work not for the usual public of concert-hall and opera-house, but for the new public that has come into being.

" He has achieved an amazing transposition of values: whence incomprehension on the part of many excellent musicians who either will not or cannot consider the work from the right angle."

Paradise Lost (based on Milton's poem, but following from start to finish an entirely different course) has also won enthusiastic, unqualified praise. The Belgian critic J. Weterings wrote of it: " Many critics found the music barbarous and disorderly. Yet, the surety of touch is marvellous, the architecture is firm, and everything in it betokens thorough ripeness of thinking and genuine originality." De Graef praised its impetuous, dramatic, deeply human character: " It is ", he concluded, " so big in its wisdom, simplicity, purity, and glow, that it mocks our puny admiration."

His Psalm for soprano and small orchestra was successfully given at Amsterdam in December 1933. A few months later it created a scandal at the Florence Festival of the International Music Society. A. de Blonay wrote of it in the *Schweizerische Musikzeitung*:

> A superb work, ripe, simple, powerful and moving. The economy of means is remarkable: no artifices, no quest for effects, nothing but essentials. Markevitch ignores the conventions of our Western music; he composes on an altogether different plane. The spirit of his music rather than the idiom is new. It expresses with extraordinary intensity an almost metaphysical anguish.

In this country, on two at least of the few occasions on which music by Markevitch was performed, no critic seems to have discovered in it either the signal qualities or the controversy-begetting elements, imponderable or not, that had been stressed on the Continent. The orchestral *Partita* (1936), accepted elsewhere as a thoroughly representative work, attracted very little notice. The concertante symphony *Le Nouvel Age* (1938), of which Kochnitsky and others had praised " the noble proportions, the sublime architecture, and the profound significance ", created an unfavourable impression. Eric Blom, one of our most experienced and fair-minded critics, declared that " this brave new world in which anything can be put down on paper as though it were of portentous significance, although anything else would be equally unpleasant and insignificant, seems to be fit only for suicides ". E. Rubbra dismissed the work as " pretentious nonsense attired with Messianic seriousness ". The present writer's view (based on first impressions, and therefore to be regarded as provisional) was that both works were competent achievements, but neither contained anything worth thinking twice about—let alone getting excited over—one way or the other.

In short, the controversial literature on Markevitch shows contrasts as sharp as that on the post-1914 works of Stravinsky. But it did not spread far, nor was it ever on a big scale. And there does not seem to be any reason to suppose that it will be, like Berlioz's or Liszt's, a lasting apple of discord; nor does it, like Scriabin's, hold out any inducement to discussion from any point of view but the purely musical.

Nikolai Nabokof (*b.* 1903, a pupil of Rebikof, and later of Hase at Strasbourg) also manifests spiritualist tendencies—not very definite, it would seem, and certainly not far-fetched—in his principal works, which are: a *Symphonie Lyrique* (1930 or thereabouts) with an epigraph consisting of a sentence from a Pushkin poem: " the soul, seething and quivering, seeks in a dream an outlet through which its torment may flow into reality " (this work was successfully performed in several countries and is said to be perspicuous, straightforward, and glowing; *Ode*, in its first form (1928), a ballet based on a poem by Lermontof, an " evening meditation on the Majesty of God on the occasion of the great aurora borealis ", remodelled in 1929 for concert performance, and said to be brilliant and imaginative; *Chants à la Vierge* for voice and piano; and an oratorio, *Job*.

Arthur Lourié (*b.* 1892, of French descent) left Petersburg— where, it would seem, none of his works had attracted much notice, possibly owing to the unfavourable conditions that prevailed at the time—for Paris in 1921. As early as 1915 he started composing sacred music, his first ventures being settings for voice and piano of French and Latin texts referring to the Blessed Virgin. His later output includes a *Regina Coeli* for contralto, oboe, and trumpet; an *Improperium* for baritone and strings; a *Sonate liturgique* for orchestra, piano, and chorus; and a *Concerto spirituel* for piano, double bass and chorus. His other principal works are a choral cantata, a ballet, *The Snow Mask*, a *Symphonie Dialectique*, an opera, *The Feast in Time of Plague*, and chamber music, including three string quartets and a sonata for violin and double bass. It has often been averred that all this deserves far greater attention than it has received.

Feodor Akimenko (*b.* 1876) was educated at St. Petersburg, and spent many years in France, but his music does not show any signs of French influence; nor is it directly related to that of any Russian except, in some of his early piano pieces, to Scriabin's. He is, by nature, fundamentally contemplative, and most of his piano music— notably the Suite *Uranie*—was inspired by natural scenery. He has composed, among other things, a symphony, a *Poème Nocturne* for orchestra, an opera, *The Little Mermaid*, and a violin concerto. A few years ago, he returned to his native Ukraine, and is now one of the members of that country's national-regional group.

Julian Krein (*b.* 1913, the son of Grigory Krein) left Russia in 1926 and studied in Paris, under Paul Dukas. His early works show a remarkable precocity—notably so a 'cello concerto, which he composed at the age of seventeen, and which bears the opus number 25. He is at his best in his orchestral music: *Lyrical Poem* for piano and orchestra, *Ballad*, and *Destruction*, a symphonic prelude in which, according to Slonimsky, he attempted to express pacifist ideas. His technique is said to be brilliant. He revels in pathetic expression, inclining to gloom. He is now settled in Russia; and we are told that he has considerably simplified his style. The latest work of his of which mention has reached us is a *Spring Symphony*.

There is no possibility of covering the activities of all the Russians working in other countries. Among those who are in the United States, the best known here are Lazar Saminsky (*b*. 1883), Alexander Tcherepnin (*b*. 1899, the son of Nikolai Tcherepnin), and Nikolai Lopatnikof (*b*. 1903). Saminsky was, at one time, one of the leaders of the Russian-Jewish nationalist group. His output includes operas, three symphonies, tone-poems, and vocal music. A. Tcherepnin, educated partly in Russia, partly in France, shows great versatility, and, according to Eric Blom (in Grove's *Dictionary*), " an exuberant gift of fantastic invention, manifested most successfully in his works on a small scale, and especially his piano music." He has composed chamber-music, concertos, an opera, *Ol-ol*, and a ballet. Lopatnikof, educated in Petersburg and in Berlin, once told a critic that he had been influenced at first by Borodin and Mussorgsky, and later by Stravinsky and Hindemith. It is in his early works, however, that affinities with Hindemith and other Central European modernists are noticeable; but these (the principal of which are a piano concerto, a string quartet, a violin sonata, and a symphony), also show a capacity for straightforward, sustained melodic invention, which manifests itself more freely in the later works ('cello sonata, second string quartet, string trio, etc.). These contain much that is genuinely Russian in character. He has composed an opera, *Danton*.

Issay Dobrowen (*b*. 1893), chiefly known as a pianist and conductor, has composed a number of works which are of the conservative order and show signs of the influence of Scriabin. Nikolai Berezovsky (*b*. 1900) is described by Slonimsky as of cosmopolitan tendencies, with distinctly nationalist features. His output includes three symphonies and chamber-music.

Vladimir Dukelsky (*b*. 1903) is widely known for his popular American music, published under the pseudonym Vernon Duke. His principal works of the serious order are a ballet, *Zephyr and Flora*, produced by Diaghilef, two symphonies (the second is described by Slonimsky in *Music since 1900* as " neo-Glinka-esque in a stylized manner "), an oratorio, *The End of St. Petersburg*, (1937), and chamber-music.

Vladimir Vogel (*b*. 1896, of a Russian father and a German

mother, educated partly in Russia, partly in Berlin) shows no inclination to use the vernacular. He was influenced by Scriabin, and later by Schönberg and to a greater degree by Busoni. He has experimented in many directions. The music of his maturity is abstract, austere, and virile. The list of his works includes orchestral music (a *Sinfonia fugata*, two Studies, entitled *Ritmica Funebre* and *Ritmica Giocosa*, *Devise*, *Tripartita*), a violin concerto, a cantata *The Fall of Wagadu* for solo voice, chorus, and five saxophones (this is interesting, and ingeniously wrought), piano music, a string quartet, a capella madrigals, and a set of variations for flute, violin, clarinet, and 'cello.

Hard   is the fate of us Christ-ians all,   op -

- pressed by the slaves of our wick - ed Tsar.

137

INDEX